Neil Dixon

Companion to the Lectionary

3. A New Collection of Prayers

EPWORTH PRESS

First published 1983
by Epworth Press
All rights reserved

Enquiries should be addressed to
Epworth Press, Room 195,
1 Central Buildings,
Westminster
London SW1H 9NR

7162 0371 5

Phototypeset by Input Typesetting Ltd
and printed in Great Britain by
The Camelot Press Ltd
Southampton

Contents

Contributors   vi
Preface   vii
Introduction   viii
For users of The Alternative Service Book   xi
Prayers   1

Contributors

Martyn D Atkins
John C A Barrett
Neil Dixon (editor)
A Raymond George
Robert W Gribben
Michael Hardstaffe
Alan E D Harvey
Richard G Jones
Ronald Lawton
Norman Revis
Donald G Rogers
Gwynneth M Spoors
Michael J Townsend
Margaret Trickett
David H Tripp
John D Walker
Ralph Waller
C Norman R Wallwork
J Richard Watson

Preface

I am most grateful to my fellow contributors, who readily accepted my invitation to them to write sets of prayers for this book and who, having submitted their work, responded positively to my editorial amendments – not without a struggle, in some cases, but always graciously. Individual styles of writing vary, of course, and no attempt has been made to force all the contributions into a common mould, though our aims and objectives, as outlined in the Introduction, were understood from the outset. This book could never have appeared without the enthusiastic involvement of the contributors, and I am deeply indebted to them.

Thanks are also due to Helen Bowness, Ros Lawton, Chris Price, Marjorie Ryan, Marie Ward and Sheila White, who worked very hard to prepare the final typescript in time to meet my deadline; and to the Rev John Stacey, Chairman of the Editorial Committee of Epworth Press, for his encouragement of the project and for many helpful suggestions.

September 1982   Neil Dixon

Introduction

The prayers in this collection have been written for use in public worship. Although there is no shortage of books of prayers on the market, there seems to be a need for prayers which are neither too short nor too long; prayers which avoid obscure or flowery language without sacrificing the rich biblical imagery that has so enhanced traditional prayers; prayers which are intelligible enough to be used with a wide range of congregations, not least when children are present, but which are not so provocatively modern as to seem out of place in worship; prayers which take account of the onward march of the lectionary without being too narrowly restricted to particular themes.

It is the hope of the contributors that this new collection will help to meet that need.

The Scope of the Prayers

A set of three prayers is provided for each Sunday and other occasion noted in the Methodist lectionary. (Users of *The Alternative Service Book* should consult the list on page ix in order to adjust the sequence of the prayers to their own lectionary requirements.)

When the Methodist lectionary presents different themes for Year 1 and Year 2, a set of prayers is offered for each year; and the great festivals of Christmas, Easter and Pentecost are provided with two sets of prayers each. Collects have been written for seven special occasions for which *The Methodist Service Book* supplies lessons but no collects; otherwise each set contains one prayer of adoration, one of confession, and one of thanksgiving and dedication.

Prayers of intercession and petition are not included. The absence of such prayers does not imply any denigration of them; they are, of course, essential elements in public prayer. But within the many books of prayers currently available, intercession and petition are already more than adequately represented. On the other hand, there appears to be a shortage of good prayers of adoration, of confession, and of thanksgiving and dedication.

Adoration, in particular, has been much neglected, and a desire to make good this deficiency is one of the principal objectives of this collection. As for confession, and also thanksgiving and dedication, though the neglect has not been so great, many published examples of these elements of prayer are too limited and specific in their scope to be adequate for use in public worship. Thus this book is restricted to those elements of prayer for which there seems to be the greatest need.

Using the Prayers

It is assumed that these prayers will normally be used in acts of worship structured as follows:

1. *The Preparation*, our approach to God. The prayers of adoration and confession are intended for use in this part of the service.
2. *The Ministry of the Word*, God's word to us in lessons and sermon.
3. *The Response*. The prayers of thanksgiving and dedication are meant to be used in this part of the service (together with intercessions and petitions and the Lord's Prayer).

Confession

It is often said, rightly, that recognition of God's forgiveness should accompany prayers of confession. The Gospel not only makes us conscious of our sin; it also assures us of God's compassion. A few of the prayers of confession in this collection are followed by a formal declaration of forgiveness, but in most cases the conviction that God forgives those who are penitent is expressed within the prayer itself. Users who prefer to make a definite statement of absolution will no doubt be aware of the excellent examples on page B6 of *The Methodist Service Book* and on page 49 of *The Alternative Service Book*. For the sake of completeness, prayers of confession are provided in every set, even though there is much to be said for the omission of confession at the three great festivals of Christmas, Easter and Pentecost.

Thanksgiving and Dedication

The contributors were asked to write prayers of thanksgiving and dedication which would be wide-ranging rather than restricted to particular themes. This policy reflects the conviction that the whole sweep of the 'salvation-history' should be celebrated, however briefly, in every prayer of thanksgiving, thus echoing the traditional eucharistic prayer. Specific thanksgivings, related to the theme of the day, can and should, week by week, find a place within a framework where the mighty acts of God in creation and redemption are recalled.

The Lord's Supper

There will normally be no need to use any of these prayers when the Lord's Supper is being celebrated. *The Methodist Service Book* (pages B5–17), or *The Alternative Service Book* (pages 119–145) will supply all that is necessary. However, in churches where the congregation turns to the service book only after the Ministry of the Word, our prayers of adoration and confession may be of use in the early part of the service. It must be emphasized that the prayers of thanksgiving and dedication should certainly *not* be used in these circumstances; for the Great Prayer of Thanksgiving (*The Methodist Service Book*, pages B12–14) or one of the Eucharistic Prayers (*The Alternative Service Book*, pages 130–141) makes any other prayer of thanksgiving redundant.

The nineteen contributors to this collection are all Methodists, and all but one are ministers or local preachers (the exception is a professor of English). They live and work in many different parts of Britain and they have wide experience as leaders of worship. These prayers arise out of that experience. We hope that the prayers will be useful to other leaders of worship, both Methodist and non-Methodist; and that, through their use, worship will be enriched and God's Name glorified.

For users of The Alternative Service Book

The Sunday themes are, for the most part, common to both *The Methodist Service Book* and *The Alternative Service Book*. In a number of instances, however, the two lectionaries differ, and users of *The Alternative Service Book* will need to consult the following list in order to find the appropriate sets of prayers.

ASB lectionary	*Appropriate Prayers*
3rd Sunday after Epiphany	3rd Sunday after Epiphany (Year 1)
4th Sunday after Epiphany	3rd Sunday after Epiphany (Year 2)
5th Sunday after Epiphany	6th Sunday after Epiphany (Year 1)
6th Sunday after Epiphany	4th Sunday after Epiphany (Year 2)
7th Sunday before Easter	4th Sunday after Epiphany (Year 1)
14th Sunday after Pentecost	15th Sunday after Pentecost
15th Sunday after Pentecost	16th Sunday after Pentecost
16th Sunday after Pentecost	14th Sunday after Pentecost
20th Sunday after Pentecost	21st Sunday after Pentecost
21st Sunday after Pentecost	6th Sunday after Epiphany (Year 2)
22nd Sunday after Pentecost	7th Sunday before Easter
Last Sunday after Pentecost	20th Sunday after Pentecost

Ninth Sunday before Christmas

Adoration

Glory and praise to God!

Eternal God, creator and sustainer of the universe,
we adore you.
Your greatness and majesty
far exceed our capacity to imagine them.
We see your glory dimly reflected
in the splendour of your creation –
in the mighty hills, the surging seas,
the beauty of flowers and the wealth of animal life.
Yet above and beyond creation, you reign supreme.

Eternal Word, Lord Jesus Christ,
we adore you.
Before all things began, you already were;
you were with the Father before the universe was made.
You became flesh and dwelt among us;
and we have seen your glory,
glory as of the only Son of the Father.

Eternal Spirit, proceeding from the Father and the Son,
we adore you.
You are the source of all beauty, all goodness, all truth.
You are ever active in creation;
you are constantly at work in us,
enabling, instructing, renewing.
You inspire and prompt our worship.

Glory and praise to God, creator, redeemer, renewer –
Father, Son, and Holy Spirit! *Amen.*

Ninth Sunday before Christmas

Confession

Great God, gracious God,
King of the universe and our creator,
we do not deserve your love.

We confess that we have too little sense of wonder:
we take for granted the beauty and majesty of your creation.
We confess that we have too little sense of responsibility:
we squander and pollute and misuse your bountiful gifts.
Not only have we failed as stewards of creation;
we have also rejected our creator.
For you have spoken, but we have not listened.
You have made known your truth, but we have ignored it.
You have revealed your love, but we have been unresponsive.

Father, forgive us.
Help us to live as faithful, grateful, responsible stewards of
    creation.
Teach us to live as obedient, responsive and loving children of our
    Father.
We ask it for the sake of Jesus Christ our Lord. *Amen.*

Thanksgiving and Dedication

Creator God, it is our duty and our joy
to give you thanks and praise.
    Yours is the mind that conceived the galaxies;
    yours the power that brought the universe into being;
    yours the love that created beauty and order.
    We worship you, we give you thanks,
    we praise you for your glory.

Father God, it is our duty and our joy
to give you thanks and praise.
    You made us in your image
    and gave us the capacity to see and appreciate
    the lovely world you made.
    We thank you that you have never abandoned us,
    though we have been faithless stewards of your bounty,
    that again and again you have shown your patient, forgiving
        love.

2

We thank you for your supreme revelation of yourself
in Jesus Christ your Son,
whose birth and ministry and death,
whose resurrection and ascension
wonderfully display your power and your purpose,
your mercy and your grace.
We thank you that, in his Name,
you have sent your life-giving Spirit
to make of us a new creation.
We worship you, we give you thanks,
we praise you for your glory.

Thankful for all your goodness,
we dedicate ourselves to your service.
Make us worthy stewards of creation,
loyal and loving children of our God;
for the sake of Jesus Christ our Lord. *Amen.*

Eighth Sunday before Christmas

Adoration

Most merciful God,
though we are members of a sinful race,
we worship and praise you for your loving kindness;
in our darkness you are the one true light,
in our sin you are our only hope,
in our weakness you alone give us strength.
Accept our praises
and continue your blessings to us, we pray,
through Jesus Christ our Lord. *Amen.*

Confession

Almighty God, our Maker and our Judge,
we have been born into a sinful world
and we ourselves are sinners.
We have sinned exceedingly in thought and word and deed.
We have marred your image in us
and fallen short of what you meant us to be.
We earnestly repent and are heartily sorry for all our misdoings.
If you, Lord, should mark iniquities,
Lord, who could stand?
But there is forgiveness with you,
steadfast love and plenteous redemption;
and you will redeem us from all our iniquities.
You sent your Son, not to condemn the world,
but that the world might be saved through him;
therefore we pray you to have mercy on us;
forgive us all that is past,
confirm and strengthen us in all goodness,
and keep us in life eternal;
for the sake of Jesus Christ our Lord and Saviour. *Amen.*

Thanksgiving and Dedication

We thank you, God our Father,
that you created the heavens and the earth
and made us in your image.

We thank you that even when we marred your image by our sin,
you sought to win us back.
You loved the world so much that you gave your only Son,
Jesus Christ, the second Adam,
who was born into the world to rescue us from the powers of evil,
and to restore what we had lost.
By his death on the Cross and his resurrection from the dead
he has opened for us the way to paradise.
At your right hand in glory he pleads our cause,
and at the last he will come to be our Judge.

Through him you have poured out the Holy Spirit,
to assure us of your forgiving love
and to make us your people,
the Church of pardoned sinners exulting in their Saviour.

As we thank you for all these mercies
we offer ourselves to you,
and pray that by your Holy Spirit
you will strengthen us in our fight against evil
and enable us to share in Christ's final victory.
We ask it in his ever-blessed Name. *Amen*.

Seventh Sunday before Christmas

Adoration

Blessed be the Lord the God of Israel,
the God of Abraham, the God of Isaac and the God of Jacob.
Blessed be his holy Name;
blessed in the highest heaven
and blessed among the people of his choice;
blessed in his glorious kingdom
and blessed in his holy Church;
blessed in time
and blessed through all eternity. *Amen.*

Confession

Most merciful God,
we confess to you the weakness of our faith
and our lack of obedience to your will;
we confess our reluctance to continue our pilgrim journey
and our slowness to put our whole trust in you.
Forgive our foolishness
and pardon our lack of dependence on your promises.
Grant us the joy of your mercy
and the assurance of your guidance in the days to come;
through Jesus Christ our Lord. *Amen.*

Thanksgiving and Dedication

Lord God, the Father of all,
with faithful Abraham
and all the families of the earth
we lift up our hearts
to bless your holy Name
for the continuance of your promises
and for the many signs of your goodness and grace.

We give you thanks for the fulfilment of your purposes
in the passion and victory of your only Son,
our Saviour, Jesus Christ;
for the power which he gives to your people
and for our calling to be your witnesses in the world.

We pray that through the gracious gifts of your Holy Spirit
we may be kept by faith and love
in the way of Christ,
and be brought at last
into the perfect obedience of your holy Word
and the blessedness of your eternal kingdom;
through Jesus Christ our Lord,
who is alive and reigns with you and the Holy Spirit,
one God, now and for ever. *Amen.*

Sixth Sunday before Christmas

Adoration

Thus says the Lord: I am who I am.

Lord almighty, everlasting, all-transcending God,
existing of yourself, uncreated, without beginning, without
 ending,
present in each place and at each moment in all the fullness of your
 perfection:
you have made us your household, under the headship of your
 beloved Son,
and in him you have made us a kingdom of priests to serve you.

Let your Spirit call forth from our hearts, we pray,
the worship befitting your splendour;
call us now to draw near with courage,
to seek your presence and speak with you,
to hear your words and obey you.
Make yourself known as our friend and our deliverer.
Glorify your Name in this hour and in all our life;
through Christ our Lord. *Amen.*

Confession

Father, you have made us your free children through the gift of
 your Son,
yet we have gone back to the foolish bondage of self-will.

You have taught us your truth, you have taught us your love,
and yet we have clung to our idols of desire, of fear, of ambition.

Father, forgive us;
hold up to our sight the sign of your love in the Cross of Christ;
let your Spirit take away from our hearts the veil of unbelief;
refresh us on our journey from the springs of your peace;
feed us in our weakness with the nourishment of your word.

Lord, let your will be done in us.
We ask this in Christ's Name. *Amen.*

Grace and truth have come through Jesus Christ.
Hear then his word of mercy to us: Your sins are forgiven.
Amen. Thanks be to God.

Thanksgiving and Dedication

God of our forebears, and God of our present age,
we praise and bless you for your great works of old:
your works of creation,
your guiding of history,
your teaching of our race.
You show us your nearness in new things and in old,
in things that endure.
You have committed yourself to our salvation,
you have set in our hearts a passion for freedom,
and have brought us liberation through the free offering of Jesus.

Now, as your Spirit moves within our being to quicken us into
    praise,
we give ourselves to you in Jesus our Lord,
who has called us by his Name, and made us his friends.
Glory be to the Father, and to the Son, and to the Holy Spirit:
as it was in the beginning, is now, and shall be for ever. *Amen.*

Fifth Sunday before Christmas

Adoration

Lord God almighty,
we praise you that in ancient times
you declared your truth to the world through Israel;
and when many of your people were faithless
you raised up a righteous remnant and spoke through fearless
    prophets.

Join us to the prophets of Israel
and all the faithful unknown who have lived in faithless times;
that with them we may praise your Name as we ought.
Above all we praise you for your Son Jesus Christ,
who was not afraid to stand alone,
and through whom we are born into the Israel of God.
Glory be to you, Lord God almighty,
now and for ever. *Amen.*

Confession

God of truth,
forgive us if we have been unwilling to stand up for your truth:
if we have refused to listen to the voices of prophets in our own
    day –
or if we have heard them and praised them,
but not taken their message to heart.

Forgive your Church
for the times when it is narrow-minded and intolerant,
refusing to hear your voice in any institution except itself.
Forgive it also
for the times when it is so receptive to other voices
that it forgets the unique place of the Lord Jesus Christ.

10

Grant us through him the knowledge that we are forgiven;
and bring the whole world to an awareness of your saving love;
for the sake of Jesus Christ our Lord. *Amen.*

Thanksgiving and Dedication

Father, we thank you that you are always active to save the world
    that you have made,
for the insights you have given us through the Old Testament
    prophets,
and for the relevance of their message to our world.

We thank you for Jesus, the greatest of prophets,
your living Word to us.
We thank you that, for our salvation,
he took our nature upon him, living our life and dying our death,
and rising again victorious.
We thank you for the gift of your Spirit
who enables your people to proclaim your message.

We thank you for all prophetic voices today;
for those who speak out against oppression in totalitarian states,
and who risk persecution, imprisonment, or even death;
for Christians – especially new and young Christians –
who make a courageous witness to your truth,
at home, at work, and among their friends.

Inspire us by the loyalty of your followers
in days of persecution and adversity,
that with them we may boldly stand up for what is true and right.
Give us such an awareness of the cloud of witnesses around us
that we may run with perseverance the Christian race.
Teach us that you never forsake those who are loyal to you,
and grant us courage and steadfastness in time of need;
for the sake of Jesus Christ our Lord. *Amen.*

Fourth Sunday before Christmas (Advent 1)

Adoration

Glory be to you, Lord God, King of the universe;
Glory be to you, Lord God, dwelling in light and majesty;
Glory be to you, Lord God, beyond our highest thoughts;
Glory be to you, Lord God, giver of light and life.
Glory be to you from the company of heaven who see you face to
　　face;
Glory be to you from your people on earth who have seen your
　　salvation.
Glory be to you, Lord God; through Jesus Christ our Lord. *Amen.*

Confession

Almighty Lord,
In Jesus you have called us to walk as children of the light;
　　but we have preferred our own way, the way of darkness;
　　we have not been willing
　　　　to let the light of Christ into every part of our lives;
　　we have not been willing
　　　　to respond with wholehearted obedience and total dedication.

Forgive us

　　because we find it easy to profess faith
　　　　but hard to translate it into action;
　　because we say so much
　　　　but do so little.

By your renewing love, grant us assurance of pardon
and strength to live up to our calling;
through Jesus Christ our Saviour. *Amen.*

Thanksgiving and Dedication

Heavenly Father,
we, your people, give you thanks and praise.

We thank you that through long years
you prepared a people to be your own.

We praise you for the patriarchs, the prophets and the lawgivers,
who brought us your words.
We rejoice in the constancy of your love,
that rebellion and indifference could not prevent you
from loving those whom you had chosen and called.

We thank you, most of all, for the coming of Jesus Christ your
    Son,
in whom your love has reached its climax and its goal.
We thank you that he is the perfect copy of your nature,
that in him we see what you are truly like.
We thank you for his birth and his ministry, his death and his
    resurrection,
his glorious revelation of your boundless love.
We thank you for all the hope and strength and courage he gives,
that we may live as you intend.

Heavenly Father, you have called us to cast off the works of
    darkness
and to walk as children of the light:
we give ourselves to this work
in the confidence that you will strengthen us in time of need.
Recreate us in the image of Jesus, we pray,
and renew us by your Holy Spirit,
that our lives may reflect the salvation Christ has brought.

We ask this, heavenly Father, in the Name of Jesus Christ our
    Lord. *Amen*.

Third Sunday before Christmas (Advent 2)

Adoration

Lord God,
yours is the imagination which conceived the whole universe,
yours the power which brings all things into being,
yours the truth which guides all life to its fulfilment in you.
We praise and adore you,
author and finisher of everything that is.

We praise you for your Word,
underlying all that exists,
giving meaning to all things that you have made,
shown to us in the story of your people,
made clear in Jesus Christ our Lord.

We praise you for all that bears witness to him,
the Word made flesh,
Saviour of all humanity,
Light of the world.
We praise you for the scriptures,
for the traditions of your Church,
for all faithful Christian living and learning.
We praise you that you have not left yourself without witness
in this age and place.

Word, Truth, Saviour, Light,
we adore you, in Jesus Christ our Lord. *Amen.*

Confession

Eternal God,
from whom alone we learn the true source,
the right way, the final goal of all life,
we confess to you our stubbornness and stupidity.
Like Adam, we run away from the sound of your voice.

We do not listen for your Word.
We do not obey our Lord.

In wilfulness we do not seek that Word
within the life of the Church,
nor in the scriptures,
nor in your speaking to our inmost spirits.
We are lazy, careless, proud, self-confident.
And so we blunder, we miss the mark, we fall short,
our lives go wrong, we hurt others.

Forgive us, Lord.

Teach us to seek, as travellers who have lost their way.
Teach us to listen, as little children to their parents.
Teach us to treasure the words,
as lovers blissful at the sound of each other's voices;
through Jesus Christ our Lord. *Amen.*

Thanksgiving and Dedication

How we thank you, Lord, for fashioning the universe
and giving us a place within it!

How we thank you for your patience with us,
despite our folly and our hard hearts!
You have not left us in our sin,
but have come to us full of grace and truth in Jesus Christ.

How we thank you for his open-ness to your calling
the power and command of his teaching,
his ministering to people's needs,
his total costly obedience to your royal way of love!
We thank you for his dying,
his rising to new life,
his freedom to reign throughout the world.

How we thank you for the life-giving energy of the Holy Spirit,
that makes Christ's work immediate to us today,
that makes his truth alive and active and full of power to save and
    guide,
that sounds his witness in our hearts!

Third Sunday before Christmas

How we thank you for the Bible,
the supreme witness to all you have done,
all you are, all that you will complete!

Take our minds, and fill them with knowledge of your whole truth.
Take our imaginations, so that we may be inspired again and again
by fresh visions of your purpose and your glory.
Take our mental powers, so that reason and memory are wholly at
    your service.
Take our wills, so that we desire only what is pleasing to you;
through Jesus Christ our Lord. *Amen.*

Second Sunday before Christmas (Advent 3)

Adoration

It is beyond our power, Father,
to put into words the wonder of your coming,
and all that it revealed and continues to reveal.
We praise you for the light that came into the world at the birth of
    your Son,
and because that light is still shining
and showing your glory to us.
No longer need we desperately hope for the best,
for we have the assurance of your love and grace.
Accept, we pray, the adoration which comes from hearts that are
    full of wonder,
a wonder words cannot express;
for the sake of Jesus Christ our Lord. *Amen.*

Confession

Lord Jesus Christ, as the anniversary of your birth draws near, we
confess that we are often too busy with our festivities to give time
to thinking about what it all means. We try to pretend that our
preparation of material things is our way of acknowledging your
birth; but deep in our hearts we know that these thoughts are
shallow and unworthy. We confess too that we sympathize
sentimentally with those less fortunate, without really doing much
to help them.

In so many ways we make Christmas less than it might be by not
giving enough thought to the real meaning of your coming.
Forgive us and help us, we pray; for your Name's sake. *Amen.*

Second Sunday before Christmas

Thanksgiving and Dedication

We thank you, Lord God, for creating the world
and for sending your Son to redeem it.
We thank you that for us he became man,
died on the Cross,
and was raised to life by your power.
We thank you that he is exalted in glory,
but ever with us through the Holy Spirit.

Especially today we thank you for John the Baptist
and all who helped to prepare the way
in the centuries before the birth of your Son;
for all who in love, service and suffering
have walked in your way ever since;
and for all who have helped us to know for ourselves
the assurance of your saving grace.

In thankfulness we dedicate ourselves
to following firmly in your way,
however hard it may be,
and to be ever ready in the service of others
who have only lately come to know the meaning of our Saviour's
    birth;
for his sake. *Amen.*

The Sunday before Christmas (Advent 4)

Adoration

Lord of all wonder and all life,
we rejoice that with you nothing is impossible.
Through you we see a vision of life in all its perfection:
prepare us for your coming in Jesus Christ,
that we may see the world as transformed by your presence and
    given meaning by your love.
Let us feel the radiance of your brightness, and not be afraid;
that we may adore you more and more,
and the world may be filled with the knowledge of your truth as the
    waters cover the sea;
through him who became a little child at Bethlehem,
our Saviour Jesus Christ. *Amen.*

Confession

Lord God, as we prepare to celebrate your coming in Jesus Christ,
we think with shame of our unworthiness. We confess that we are
not ready to receive your Son, and never will be. We have thought
too highly of ourselves, and have forgotten how foolish and
inadequate we are: we have been proud when we should have
been humble, and thought ourselves mighty when we were weak.
We ask you to forgive us, Lord God, for all our sins, especially our
conceit and pride: help us to understand that we are wrong, not
only in our actions, but also in our attitudes of mind. Help us to
remember that your forgiving love, in the coming of Jesus Christ,
is needed to overcome our folly and wickedness; help us to see the
Child, born in a poor stable, as a new hope for us all; and help us
to be more honest with ourselves, more truthful about our sins,
and more loving to our fellow men and women; through Jesus
Christ our Lord and Saviour. *Amen.*

The Sunday before Christmas

Thanksgiving and Dedication

Heavenly Father, who chose the foolish things of this world to confound the wise, and the weak things of this world to confound the mighty: we bless and praise your holy Name for all your goodness to us, and especially for the hope that is ours in the birth of Jesus Christ.

We remember that the angel Gabriel was sent to a humble girl whose name was Mary, and we ask you likewise to use us, even us, in your providence and your mercy. We thank you for the yearly message of the Child, born in the stable, and for the hope that comes to us through his life. We thank you for the sure and certain knowledge that in him you became man, that he lived a human life, died on the Cross, and was raised again victorious, that through him you have sent us your Holy Spirit as guide and comforter.

Take us and use us, we pray; give us confidence that we are a part of your purpose for the world; and rouse us to a sense of our glorious calling as children of God; through Jesus Christ our Lord. *Amen.*

Christmas Day
(*1st set*)

Adoration

Eternal God,
in your mind life had its beginning:
you moulded mankind from the earth
and breathed your Spirit into us.
You know and understand
the purpose of human life.

You made us for each other,
and when we love
your love is born again in us.
The tenderness of parenthood
is part of your design:
the love of Mary for her Son
a parable of your care for us.
These signs we see with our human eyes
and respond to what we know;
but the greatness of your love
is beyond our power to imagine:
your compassion for your creation
is infinite and eternal.
By faith you enable us to see
that in the Child born at Bethlehem
you have placed yourself in our hands.

God-with-us,
we praise you for Jesus,
in whom your creation comes to perfection.

Glory to you, loving Father;
glory to you, living Son;
glory to you, enlivening Spirit;
one God for ever and ever. *Amen.*

Christmas Day

Confession

Father,
on this day you challenge us with your love:
'Beloved, if God so loved us,
we ought also to love one another.'

Your love knows no limits;
our love is partial.
Your love reaches all mankind;
we love our friends and choose our neighbours.
Your love is inexhaustible;
our charity begins and ends at home.

We are sorry that so little of your love
has reached others through us.

Touch, heal and restore us.
Make us again your strong sons and daughters,
partners in a new humanity,
born of God,
in Jesus Christ our Lord. *Amen*.

Thanksgiving and Dedication

Creator Lord,
you brought the universe into being
and in Jesus
the mysterious wisdom which all seek
is uttered in a single word.
We thank you that we have heard it!

In Jesus,
the great light which illuminates the world
is focused in a single life.
We thank you that we have seen it!

In Jesus,
the power for every task under heaven
is poured out in your Spirit.
We thank you that we have felt it!

Father,
we thank you for Jesus,
the hope of all humanity:
he taught us how to live and how to die;
he showed us the true meaning
of faithfulness, obedience and compassion.
We thank you for those who brought us to him;
for those who have guided us
and lessened our loneliness;
for those who encourage us
to keep on loving
when we despair of mankind.

We open ourselves again to you:
create us anew in your Son
and give us your word and your Spirit
that we may be children of light
and witness the coming of your kingdom,
this day and for ever. *Amen*.

Christmas Day
(2nd set)

Adoration

Lord God, your kingdom is infinite and your glory beyond our
    imagining.
Your Word brought order out of chaos;
and the light of your Word continues to shine in places that are
    dark.
We bring you our worship and praise.

Heavenly Father, today we gasp in wonder
that you have chosen to come to our world
in the form of Jesus, your Son,
that we might more clearly see your love in action,
and your power over evil, sin and death.

Lord Jesus Christ, born for us at Bethlehem,
we praise you that you are ever with us by your Spirit,
prompting us to find in you, the way;
leading us to yourself, the truth;
and seeking to be born in us
to bring new life.

Almighty God, ruler of the universe,
yet born into our world in Christ,
you inspire us to wonder and adore. *Amen.*

Confession

We come before you, Father,
knowing that your Son Jesus Christ
was rejected by the world,
even at his birth;
and we remember with shame
the ways in which we have rejected him.

We have failed to recognize your Word,
spoken to us in him;
we have spurned his way of love
and chosen to follow our own selfish instincts;
we have been too proud to enter the stable
where we would find the true riches
Christ entered the world to share.

Forgive us, too, Father,
that we have failed to acknowledge
that you can take the small and ordinary things of life,
as you did at Bethlehem,
and use them for your glory.

Grant us your pardon, and fill us with your grace;
for the sake of Jesus Christ our Lord. *Amen.*

Thanksgiving and Dedication

For the joys of home; for gatherings of family and friends; for the
young with their simplicity and enthusiasm; for parents with all
their responsibilities; and for the old with all their happy
memories:
for these your mercies,
we give you thanks.

For the joys of celebration; for all the greetings we have received;
for friendships revived and renewed; for parties to attend; for
special food, decorations and bright lights; and for those about
us to share our rejoicing:
for these your mercies,
we give you thanks.

For the gifts we have received; for our comforts and pleasures; but
supremely for your gift to us of your Son, Jesus Christ, our Lord
and our Saviour; for his coming as a child to melt our hearts; for
his living and dying and rising; for the new life and joy and peace
we find in him:
for these your mercies,
we give you thanks.

Christmas Day

Lord God, your Son seems so small and vulnerable as he enters the world this Christmas, and yet we know that people from all races have come to recognize him as King of kings and Lord of lords. Accept the worship and devotion that we bring in his Name; and use us to further the kingdom of love which he came on earth to establish; for his sake. *Amen.*

The Sunday after Christmas

Adoration

Eternal God, we worship you in your greatness,
   in the universe which we cannot comprehend,
   with the sun and moon and stars
   which remind us of your distance from us.

And yet we recall
   that a star led the wise men to Bethlehem,
   and to your Son;

and we rejoice
   that in the birth of Jesus, we see you,
   stooping, guiding, directing,
   God with us.

Eternal God, we worship you in your greatness.
We worship you too in your nearness,
our eternal light and guide. *Amen.*

Confession

Eternal God, we confess that we have not been faithful to the truth
   which you have revealed to us.
We have seen the Star, but have followed with faltering steps.
We have come, with wise men and shepherds,
the great and the humble, to worship;
but we are obsessed by our own concerns;
burdened by our worries,
and distracted by our worldliness.

As we come to worship today, we pray that you will yet receive us,
mixed in our motives, but conscious of our needs.
Forgive us our preoccupation with ourselves
and our indifference to the needs of others.

The Sunday after Christmas

Grant that, as we worship,
we may find light and strength
and forgiveness for our sins;
for the sake of Jesus Christ our Lord. *Amen.*

Thanksgiving and Dedication

Father God, we thank you for creating the universe
and making us in your own image.
We thank you that, when we plunged into the darkness of sin,
you did not abandon us, but sent your Son to be our Saviour.
In his birth and his life, in his death and his resurrection,
we see the shining of the one true Light,
we glimpse your eternal glory.

We thank you, Father, that you guided wise men from the East
to worship at our Saviour's birth.
We thank you for the wisdom of every generation
which has been offered in your service,
for the light which has been shed on your purpose for us.
We thank you for the wise and the good,
for those who have sought peace in the midst of war
and love in the face of hatred;
for those who have enriched our lives
by their words and music, their ideas and their deeds.
We thank you for those in former days, and in our own day,
who have faithfully followed the Light of the world,
witnessing to truth,
bringing hope,
sharing Christ's love and suffering.
We pray that today you will kindle a flame of love in our hearts,
that we may bring light and warmth
into lives that are dark and cold;
to the glory of your holy Name. *Amen.*

Second Sunday after Christmas
(*Year 1*)

Adoration

Almighty Father,
with your servant Hannah
who prayed silently in her heart
for a son,
and in due time presented Samuel
to you in the temple,
our hearts exult in you,
and we rejoice in your salvation.

We remember too the joy of your servant Simeon
whose prayer to see the Lord's Christ
was answered
when Mary brought her Son to the temple:
according to your word,
your salvation is before our eyes,
a light to reveal you to all peoples
and glory to your own people Israel.

We worship you, loving, listening God.
We present our prayers and praises
before your presence,
drawn to your light,
seeking your way;
through Jesus Christ our Lord. *Amen.*

Confession

Father of all,
you have revealed yourself to all who can see
in the light of Jesus Christ.

Second Sunday after Christmas

You spoke to us in human form
so that we could hear and understand you,
see and follow you.

We would rather live in the darkened room
of our own wisdom,
finding our way by common sense,
stumbling along with our own philosophy of life.

Pardon the poverty of our vision
and raise our sights to see your glory.
Set our feet firmly in the way of Christ,
and guide us to be his faithful followers.
Open our ears to hear your word
and our mouths to interpret you,
that others may recognize your truth
and walk with us,
as prophets of your coming kingdom;
through Jesus Christ our Lord. *Amen*.

Thanksgiving and Dedication

God of power and love,
we depend on your creation
and thrive on its goodness.
You answer our ingratitude
with the gift of your Son:
born as one of us,
he lived our life
and died our death;
by raising him to glory
you made us a new creation
to sing your praise.

We thank you, God our Father,
for every sign of your activity amongst us,
and especially for the company of Christ
in his living Body, the Church.
We thank you for the variety of gifts
your Spirit gives us to build us up:
gifts of understanding and service,
of teaching and counselling,
of generosity and active love.

We thank you for the different parts we play,
members of one Body,
belonging to each other,
equally blessed by your grace.

By your mercy in Christ
we offer ourselves to be living prayers,
servants of your Spirit in time and space.
Transform our minds and bind us to you
that we may show
what is the good and acceptable and perfect will of God;
through Jesus Christ our Lord. *Amen.*

Second Sunday after Christmas
(*Year 2*)

Adoration and Confession

Lord God, high and lifted up,
we bow before you.
Heavenly Father, whose love reaches down to us,
we offer you our praise.

Lord and Saviour, you are present in the world you have made,
and we worship you.
We praise you that through the weakness and helplessness of a
    child,
your greatness and power are demonstrated to the world;
that the darkness of our hearts is illuminated by his light;
that the ignorance of our minds is disturbed by his questioning and
    his wisdom.

We praise you, Lord God,
that in Jesus you come to reverse what is wrong,
and to lead your people
in ways of peace, of fellowship and of fulfilment.

But we confess, most merciful Father,
that we have sinned against heaven and before you,
and are not worthy to be called your children.
Do not condemn us, but cleanse us from our sins;
do not despise our weakness, but give us your strength;
do not leave us in darkness, but open our eyes to your light;
do not abandon us in our ignorance and self-satisfaction, but
    challenge our minds and hearts, and lead us towards your truth.

So, Father, help us to share in your desire
that righteousness shall conquer in your world and in our hearts,
that we may find meaning for ourselves
in the coming and growing of Jesus.
We ask it in his Name. *Amen.*

Thanksgiving and Dedication

Lord God, creator of the changing world
and of the human mind,
we thank you for placing in all of us
the need to question and to understand.

We thank you that in Jesus
we see one who grew and developed,
who sought your guidance throughout his life,
and was responsive to your leading.
We thank you for his questioning spirit
and his thirst for knowledge;
for his sacrifice for us upon the Cross
and his triumphant resurrection.

We thank you for
   discoveries by scientists and technologists
   who work with the physical materials of the world;

   the creative expression of artists
   in materials, words, music and movement,
   which give a deeper insight into the human condition;

   social scientists who seek to understand
   human behaviour and relationships;

   and for your Holy Spirit,
   who breathes through every manifestation of human knowledge
      and creativity.

So, Father, we offer ourselves to you.
Help us to seize our present opportunities
to grow and to serve you,
that, by exercising the talents you have given us,
we may meet physical, mental and spiritual needs
in others and ourselves,
through the Holy Spirit working within us;
for the sake of Jesus Christ our Lord. *Amen.*

Epiphany

Eternal God, yours is the greatness,
the power, the majesty, the splendour and the glory;
for everything in heaven and on earth is yours.

We worship and adore you; we bless and praise your holy Name.

Throughout the ages
you have revealed to men and women glimpses of your glory –
the glory that was fully manifest in Jesus Christ our Lord.

For he is your eternal Word, the source of life and light.
That light shines on in the darkness
and darkness has never been able to quench it.
The Word became flesh and lived among us;
and we have seen his glory, full of grace and truth.

Eternal God, revealed to us in Jesus,
we worship and adore you; we bless and praise your holy Name;
through Jesus Christ our Lord. *Amen.*

Confession

Forgive us, Lord,
> that we have been preoccupied with our own concerns
> and oblivious to the revelation of your glory;

as we pass from one year to another we

> that we have been led by our own impulses and desires
> and failed to follow your guiding light;

> ⌈ that we have been dazzled by the tinsel wrappings of Christmas
> ⌊ and blind to the Baby who is the Light of the world.

34

As we draw near to him today,
we pray that, like the wise men of old,
we may see the light of your glory shining in his face,
and bow down and worship him;
for his sake. *Amen.*

Thanksgiving and Dedication

God our heavenly Father,
we thank you for the universe
and for all living things that you
have created and sustained;
for making us in your own image,
so that we find our fulfilment
only as we walk in the light of your presence.

When we preferred darkness,
you did not abandon us to it,
but sent your Son to show us the way back to your light.
Through his birth, his life, his death and his resurrection,
he revealed the full extent of your love for everyone.

We thank you that, at his birth,
not only shepherds of Judea,
but also wise men from the East
came to pay him homage;
that, in the infant Jesus,
Simeon recognized not only the glory of his people Israel
but also the Light that lightens the gentiles;
that, throughout his life,
his compassion went out to all in need;
that he died on the Cross for the salvation of all;
that he is risen and alive and at work, through the Holy Spirit,
in his world,
in the Church which is his Body,
and in the hearts of all who love him.

Father, as we think of your great giving to us,
we humbly offer to you our gifts, our hearts, ourselves,
and pray that, in the power of the Spirit,
we may live and work to your praise and glory;
for the sake of Jesus Christ our Lord. *Amen.*

First Sunday after Epiphany

Adoration

Father God, we worship you.
We wonder at the way you choose such simple things
to reveal your power and glory.

You chose a humble Jewish home to be the birthplace of Jesus,
the Saviour of the world;
a river of water as the place to manifest
the nature and mission of your Son;
a cross of wood, as the means by which you might declare
your power and your love.

We adore you for the way you have come to us in Jesus,
and quickened the ordinariness of our existence
with your renewing Spirit.

We praise you, Father God,
that you still make all things new;
through Jesus Christ our Lord. *Amen*.

Confession

We rejoice, Father,
that in baptism you have called us to new life
and assured us that the old can be put away.

We confess our need to be made new by your Spirit,
for we have been so concerned with our own selfish desires
that we have failed to notice the concerns of others.
We have been so involved with trivial things
that we have lost our hope and trust in you
who can transform us and make us new.

We confess our need to know again
your purifying love,
which causes us to rejoice in the knowledge
that by your word of forgiveness
we are made whole.

Forgive us, Father,
and help us to live
as those who have died to sin
and risen with Christ to new life.
We ask it for his sake. *Amen*.

Thanksgiving and Dedication

Almighty and eternal God,
we thank you that you created the universe
and that you have revealed yourself to us in human form
in Jesus Christ your Son, our Lord.

We thank you that he chose to identify himself
with us and all mankind,
and accepted baptism in water
as the means by which he might declare your will and purpose
and be filled with the Holy Spirit.

We thank you for the mission of love
which Christ's baptism inaugurated;
for his offering of himself upon the Cross;
for his mighty resurrection and his glorious ascension.

We thank you that our baptism has united us with Christ,
incorporated us into his mission,
and made us part of his body, the Church.

We thank you that, as by baptism we share in Christ's death,
so by your grace we share in his victory over death.

We thank you that you still dwell within us,
refreshing us by your Spirit,
and making us able to serve you
in the world Christ came to save.

First Sunday after Epiphany

Almighty and eternal God,
you have made us yours by baptism and the Holy Spirit:
we offer ourselves again to you,
and pray that we may be your faithful soldiers and servants
to our life's end;
in the Name of Jesus Christ our Lord. *Amen.*

Second Sunday after Epiphany

Adoration

Almighty God,
we acknowledge your voice in all creation.
You spoke; and the universe came into being;
you spoke; and gave form and purpose to its life.
At your word the men and women of old began in faith to discover
     your truth.
In Jesus your Word became flesh,
and your loving purpose was revealed in tangible form.
Through him you called together the first disciples
and enabled them to receive your Holy Spirit,
moulding them into your Church.

We believe that you speak still,
calling even people like us to your service.
Open our minds, and our hearts, to what you are saying to us now,
that we may more clearly understand your purpose
and more truly serve you;
through Jesus Christ our Lord. *Amen.*

Confession

Lord, we bring to you our prayers of confession.
Because you know us through and through,
you already know our failures, and our need of your forgiveness,
but we believe that by naming them we open ourselves to your
     healing
and we are confident that you are willing and waiting to forgive
and to lead us to a new beginning.
So we confess to you the poverty of our discipleship,
our arrogance which makes us unable to learn your way and your
     truth,
the complacency with which we view our own feeble efforts.

Second Sunday after Epiphany

We confess our lack of faith, and hope, and love.
We confess our failure to be fully open to your call,
and to be whole-hearted in our response.
(Silence)
Lord, forgive us, as you forgave your disciple Peter when he failed
    you.
Call us again to your service;
teach us, heal us, and send us to live as your disciples;
for your Name's sake. *Amen.*

Thanksgiving and Dedication

We thank you, eternal God,
for every way in which you teach us your nature and your purpose.

We thank you that you taught your people Israel
that you are one God, creator and Lord of all;
you gave them your commandments, and led them to discover
    your will.

We thank you that Jesus came among us,
human as we are, yet perfectly revealing you to us;
that he taught your way of love,
and called people to live in your kingdom;
that in fulfilment of his commitment to your will
he gave himself up for us,
even to die upon the Cross.

We thank you that you raised him in triumph,
and have given him such glory
that he is to be worshipped and honoured as Lord and God.

We thank you that the first disciples left everything to follow him,
and became the first stewards of the Gospel.
We thank you that, in obedience,
they travelled far and wide, facing great danger and hardship,
to preach and teach in his Name.
We thank you that you have sent your Holy Spirit
to inspire and bless their work
and to lead us into your truth.

We thank you that you call us to be disciples too.
Help us as we follow Jesus,
and equip us to share in the task of making disciples of all the
  nations;
for the sake of Jesus Christ our Lord. *Amen.*

Third Sunday after Epiphany
(*Year 1*)

Adoration

Lord our God, we adore your Name and nature.

By Name you are the mysterious One,
always and everywhere present.
You make yourself known to us,
yet shield us from the realization of your full splendour
for we would be overwhelmed by your glory.
We are sometimes able to trace your influence on our lives
by looking back,
but we cannot presume to know the ways in which your love will
   bless us
for you are free to act as you will.

By nature you are gracious and compassionate.
You know us all by name
and your personal love has been declared to us
and promised to us in baptism.
We have become part of your distinctive people, the Church,
and we enjoy your undeserved favour.

May your heavenly glory touch and transform our human nature
so that we may be changed from glory into glory
and enter that realm of wonder, love and praise which is without
   end;
for the sake of Jesus Christ your Son our Lord. *Amen.*

Confession

We confess to you, almighty God,
that we have run after passing pleasures
and forfeited the gift of real joy.

At times we have withdrawn from participation
in the common family life of the Church,
without realizing that such life is shared with you.
We have not always heard or obeyed Christ implictly,
preferring our own inclinations to his promptings through the Holy
   Spirit.
And so our lives have become tasteless.

We long for the royal wine of the kingdom,
enjoyed in fellowship and obedience together.
As we worship, may we know that we are forgiven;
assure us of your continuing presence and patience with us;
and grant us joy and peace within;
through Jesus Christ our Lord. *Amen*.

Thanksgiving and Dedication

We thank you, God our Father, for revealing yourself to us.
You have given us glimpses of your glory
through the soft and savage beauty of your world.
You convince us of your greatness by the starry sweeps of space.

We thank you for making your purposes of love more explicit
in and through our Lord Jesus Christ.
In him your love has been focused in a life that could be seen,
words that could be heard,
and a person who could be touched.
For us he lived and died and rose again,
and reigns with you in glory;
yet he is ever present with us through the Holy Spirit.

For such awesome condescension we praise you,
and ask that we may share in the continuing revelation of your love
   to the world.
Bring us to share in the bridal feast of Christ and his Church
when heaven and earth combine in joy.
In his Name we ask it. *Amen*.

Third Sunday after Epiphany
(Year 2)

Adoration

Almighty God, whom the heaven of heavens cannot contain,
we rejoice that we can bring our prayers of adoration before you,
unworthy though they be.
You are wonderful and glorious beyond our imagining,
and yet your love encompasses the smallest creature.
We are amazed beyond telling when we consider your creative
    activity–
the mighty mountains, the tiniest flower;
but above all we marvel that you created us in your own image
and redeemed us in Christ when we fell into sin.
How could we fail to offer you our praise
when we think on these things?
Hear us, we pray,
for Christ's sake. *Amen.*

Confession

We are sorry, Father God, that we are so engrossed with ourselves
and our own concerns that we do not give time to considering why
you made us who we are and put us where we are. Sometimes we
feel that our affairs are too trivial to bother you with, or that we
can manage our lives by ourselves. And yet we know that we are
part of your kingdom; that you created us and have a purpose for
us. Forgive our self-centredness, and give us a wider vision, so that
in you we may find our true selves and the reason for our being.
We ask it through Jesus Christ our Lord. *Amen.*

Thanksgiving and Dedication

God our Father, we thank you for all the benefits you have bestowed on us; for the things we all share – the air we breathe, the world of nature. We thank you for Jesus Christ, the sure foundation of our faith, who lived and died and rose again to bring us eternal life. We thank you for the work of your Holy Spirit, dwelling within us, enabling us to worship and serve you.

Today we thank you especially for the gift of our human bodies; remembering that they are your temples, we seek your help in caring for them as your dwelling-place. We thank you for the particular abilities with which you have endowed us; help us to use them to the full, in the service of our fellow men and women, to your glory.

We thank you too for those other temples, our churches; we would care for them and have them stand as worthy witnesses to a living faith. So may we dedicate ourselves to the honour of your Name; for the sake of Jesus Christ our Lord. *Amen.*

Fourth Sunday after Epiphany
(Year 1)

Adoration

Almighty Father, we turn to you,
for you alone are our God,
the fount of everlasting wisdom,
the light of our lives, the soul of our souls,
with whom faithful people of every age
have found love and life and friendship.

Our minds cannot hold you, our words cannot express you,
for your light and loveliness are beyond our understanding.
And yet you have been our guide and companion
over every mountain and through every dark valley of our
    experience.

Today we offer you our worship
and lift our hearts to you in praise and adoration;
through Jesus Christ our Lord. *Amen.*

Confession

God our Father, we turn from the noisy arena of life,
with its trouble and anxiety,
to you, the living God;
and we confess that we come into the shadow of your presence
as those who are sick and in need of a physician,
as those who are lonely and in need of a friend,
as those who are sinners in need of a Saviour.

Forgive us that we have so often been useless to you,
that we have disobeyed your command
and acted in an unloving way towards others.

Forgive us if we have complained about our circumstances
instead of rejoicing in your love.
Forgive us that we have failed to be the people you intended us to
      be.

Out of the depths of our hearts we cry to you:
Lord God, hear our prayer.
May your grace and peace come into our lives
and lead us from a life of slavery and sin
into a life of freedom and joy and love;
through Jesus Christ our Lord. *Amen.*

Thanksgiving and Dedication

Almighty God, we are full of gratitude for all your goodness to us.
Deep in our hearts we feel a great sense of thankfulness.
We thank you for friends, whose loyalty and love have supported
      our lives,
for the opportunities that have called us forward to new
      adventure,
for the wealth of truth and beauty that has enriched our lives.
We thank you for the life and witness of loved ones
who have gone on into the unseen world.

Above all, we thank you for Jesus Christ, the Friend of sinners,
for his life of love, his death on the Cross,
his glorious resurrection and his friendship to us and to everyone.

We thank you that, by the power of the Spirit,
Christ's invitation, Follow me, has come to men and women down
      through the ages.

May we too rise up and follow him.
Inspire our work and our prayer,
and fill us with your grace and peace.
So may we walk in the steps of him
who came to seek and to save that which was lost.
We ask this in the Name of Jesus Christ our Lord. *Amen.*

Fourth Sunday after Epiphany
(Year 2)

Adoration

Living God, the giver of life,
we worship and adore you.
You commanded all things into existence;
and gave humanity its first breath;
even now you are at work in your world,
creating, sustaining, renewing.
New life is your never-ending gift to us.
Creating, sustaining, life-giving God,
we praise and adore you,
in the Name of Jesus Christ our Lord. *Amen.*

Confession

Father, we are not satisfied with our lives;
we live as though you were not with us.
Forgive our failure to accept the abundant life
offered to us in Jesus Christ.
You know our lives;
you know our dissatisfaction with them.
We long for them to be better;
we need your life-changing power.
Give us grace to amend our lives
and strengthen our resolve to follow you.
So may we live the abundant life
which you have promised can be ours;
through Jesus Christ our Lord. *Amen.*

Thanksgiving and Dedication

God our Father, we thank you for the gift of life:
for the creation and preservation of the earth,
and for the opportunities we have to share in your purposes
as stewards of creation.

We thank you for Jesus Christ, for his grace toward us,
and his offer of eternal life to all people.
His abundant life betrays the poverty of our living,
yet inspires us to live like him;
his death demonstrates his love for us all;
his resurrection makes plain your transforming power;
his ascension offers us hope in the kingdom prepared for us.

We thank you that, through your Holy Spirit,
we can be strengthened to live like Jesus,
to love him,
and to experience your power and the increase of hope;
for he brings to us the fullness of new life in Christ.

We yield our lives to you – bodies, minds, and spirits.
Remake us by your Holy Spirit's power,
that we may be enabled to live the life to which you call us;
through Jesus Christ our Lord. *Amen.*

Fifth Sunday after Epiphany *(Year 1)* and
Twenty-third Sunday after Pentecost *(Year 2)*

Adoration

Almighty God, our heavenly Father,
creator and renewer of all that is,
we praise you for all the gifts that you have showered upon us.
We praise you for the beauty we see around us,
for the infinite variety of your creation,
and for the unexpected and the surprising
which add richness to our daily life.

We praise you for your love which sustains and renews us,
and we offer you our worship and our love;
in the Name of Christ our Lord. *Amen.*

Confession

Father God, we know that you offer us new life in Christ,
but still we shut your Spirit out of our hearts and our lives.
We have tried to live in our own way,
and in our own strength;
we have strayed far away from the paths that you want us to tread.

Forgive us, Father God.
Take our failures,
our half-hearted efforts,
and our selfish prayers;
and by the power of your Holy Spirit
transform our insipid lives
into the rich new wine of your kingdom;
through Jesus Christ our Lord. *Amen.*

Thanksgiving and Dedication

Heavenly Father,
we your servants give you thanks
on this day of resurrection and new life.
You have created us;
your providence sustains us;
and your loving arms embrace us and all our brothers and sisters of
    many nations.

We thank you for the supreme gift of human history,
the gift of your Son Jesus Christ.
We thank you that he knew the love of an ordinary human family,
the affection of friends,
and the joys and sorrows of daily living.
We thank you for his ministry, his death and his resurrection,
and for the new life which he gives to those who have faith in him
    today.

We thank you for the gift of the Holy Spirit,
who every day renews us, guides us, and enables us.

We offer our lives to you in gratitude and in faith,
asking that you will use each one of us
in the service of your kingdom;
through Jesus Christ our Lord. *Amen.*

Fifth Sunday after Epiphany *(Year 2)* and
Twenty-third after Pentecost *(Year 1)*

Adoration

We praise you, Lord God our Father,
creator and sustainer of the universe.
You never slumber nor sleep, you never falter nor fail,
and you are never false to your own nature.

We praise you, Lord Jesus Christ.
You shared in the Father's work of creation,
and you finished the work he gave you to do
for the salvation of the world.

We praise you, Lord God the Holy Spirit.
You are alive and active,
in the Christian individual, in the Church, and in the world.

Let the work of your people this day
be to bring honour and glory to your Name,
Lord God, the Father, the Son and the Holy Spirit. *Amen.*

Confession

Forgive us, Father, for our lack of integrity and industry in our
daily work; for our ingratitude for the work that others are doing
on our behalf; and for our little concern for the unemployed and
exploited in every land. Pardon us for those times when we excuse
ourselves from voluntary work by saying that we are too busy, and
for the times when we are so involved in voluntary work that we
neglect home and family life.

May we hear your word of forgiveness from him who worked as a
carpenter at Nazareth, Jesus Christ your Son our Lord. We ask it
in his Name. *Amen.*

Thanksgiving and Dedication

God our Father, we thank you for your work of creation
and for your constant providential care.
We thank you that your Son,
who came among us, lived our life, died our death, and is risen and
    exalted,
shared our human life and work,
to give dignity to labour
and to redeem our working life from selfishness.

We thank you for all who work cheerfully and honestly,
all who have striven for better conditions for workers,
and all who are active today
to bring to workers in the developing world
the benefits we take for granted.

We offer you our daily work,
that we may do it to your honour and glory.
We offer you our leisure time,
that we may use it wisely and well.
We offer you our life together in your Church,
that we may believe and worship, serve and witness as we ought.

May we always be trustworthy, dependable, unselfish, and kind,
following the example of Jesus Christ your Son, our Lord;
for his sake. *Amen.*

Sixth Sunday after Epiphany *(Year 1)* and
Twenty-second Sunday after Pentecost *(Year 2)*

Adoration

Lord our God,
on this your day
we enter your house
to rejoice in your presence
with the gladness of your Gospel
within our hearts;
before the whole choir of heaven
and in the company of this congregation,
enable us, in the power of your Holy Spirit,
to praise your holy Name
and to acknowledge the majesty of your glory,
for ever and ever. *Amen.*

Confession

Most gracious and most merciful God,
we confess to you
and to one another
that time after time we have entered your presence
with countless prayers
but with hearts that have been closed to your grace;
we have lifted our hands to you in praise
but our feet have still walked in the ways of evil;
we have rehearsed your commandments
but have refused to see your face
in the needs of our neighbour.
We pray you, Lord, to forgive our lack of faith
and to pardon our acts of injustice;
grant us the healing that comes from your presence
and the cleansing of your all-powerful word;

54

through Jesus Christ our Lord. *Amen.*

Thanksgiving and Dedication

Wisdom of the Most High,
we praise and magnify your holy Name
for your enduring goodness
whereby you have granted the glory of your presence
to your people.
We bless you for your powerful acts
in the creation of the universe,
and in the sending of redemption to your people
through the incarnation and exaltation of your only-begotten Son,
our Saviour, Jesus Christ.
We bless you for the out-pouring of your Spirit,
for the foundation of your holy Church
and for its perpetual ministry of praise and prayer.
Grant, that walking in the way of your commandments,
we may be kept firm for ever
in your righteousness and truth
and rejoice in your holiness all the days of our life;
through Jesus Christ our Lord,
to whom with you, Father, and the Holy Spirit,
we ascribe all honour and glory,
now and for ever. *Amen.*

Sixth Sunday after Epiphany *(Year 2)* and
Twenty-second Sunday after Pentecost *(Year 1)*

Adoration

All-powerful and everliving God,
most blessed and most holy,
before the brightness of whose presence
the angels veil their faces:
we are not worthy to lift up our eyes to your glory,
and yet you are pleased to accept our worship.
Blessing and glory and wisdom and thanksgiving
and honour and power and might
be to our God for ever. *Amen.*

Confession

God our Father, through your Son
you have bidden us worship you in spirit and in truth.
We confess the irreverence and insincerity
which often mar our worship;
we praise you with our lips,
but our thoughts are far from you.

Help us to approach you with awe and reverence
and to rejoice that you are the merciful and loving Father of our
    Lord Jesus Christ.
Forgive us, we pray, for his sake. *Amen.*

Thanksgiving and Dedication

All glory to you, Lord our God,
for you created the heavens and the earth
and formed us in your own image.

56

No one has ever seen you,
but your only Son has made you known
and in his face we have seen your glory.
He lived and died as one of us,
to reconcile us to you.
He stretched out his arms on the Cross
and offered himself in obedience to your will,
a perfect sacrifice for the whole world.

In this our sacrifice of praise and thanksgiving
we recall his death, his resurrection, his ascension, and his
    continual prayer for us in heaven;
and we offer ourselves to you as a living sacrifice.
Accept us, we pray,
for the sake of Jesus Christ our Saviour;
fulfil your will in us by the power of your Holy Spirit,
and bring us and all people to the heavenly Jerusalem
and to the assembly of the first-born who are enrolled in heaven.
We ask this through him who is the mediator of the new covenant,
Jesus Christ our Saviour. *Amen.*

Ninth Sunday before Easter
(Education Sunday)

Adoration

Hear the word of the Lord:
The time is fulfilled, the kingdom of God is at hand.
Repent; and believe the Good News.

Let us be quiet before God,
and by our stillness acknowledge his divine presence.
(Silence)

Holy God, holy and mighty, holy and gracious,
your children draw near to adore you in this house of your mercy.
As you sent us your Son to reveal your kingdom,
speak with us now in him, your eternal Word.
Lead our longings to the joy of knowing you,
our wills to the glad obedience of your reign.
Make us truly one with each other and with all who worship you,
that in prayer and in life we may be a people for your praise
in Jesus Christ our Lord. *Amen.*

Confession

The kingdom of God is at hand, says the Lord.
Repent; and believe the Good News.

Humbly we offer God our penitence.

Father, through your law and through our conscience,
through the life and words of Jesus,
you have taught us how far we are astray,
how much your children need your pardon and your discipline.
In Jesus' Name we come to you and ask to be forgiven
for our small faith, for our failure in Christian caring and witness,
for being so slow to obey Christ, so timid in learning new tasks of
   love.

Give us new hope in your Son, new courage in your Spirit,
new life in your service;   for Christ's sake. *Amen.*

The Lord Jesus says to us:
The words I have spoken to you, they are spirit and they are life.
Hear then his word of grace to us: Your sins are forgiven.
Amen. Thanks be to God.

Thanksgiving and Dedication

Lord Jesus Christ, you have come to bring us truth,
to shine in our darkness,
to point for us the way from death to life;
you have sown the seed of hope in the soil of our history:
in your living and your loving, in your death and resurrection,
you have undermined our pride and taught us a new dignity of
    service.

As you gathered your first disciples around you on the hill-side,
you have been in our midst as we worshipped,
and you have confronted us in your word.
For this, Lord Christ, we bless you.

By the Spirit's guidance,
open our minds to more and more of your truth,
our hearts and hands to more of the need of your world.
Make us, your disciples, one in your Name,
a living sacrifice to your heavenly Father,
that with our neighbours we may learn from you his will;
for with him and the Spirit you are one God in truth and for ever
    and ever. *Amen.*

Eighth Sunday before Easter

Adoration

We worship you, eternal God,
creator of the universe, source of all being,
sustainer of all life.

We stand amazed in your presence,
whose glory and power are great beyond our imagining.
The blazing light of your purity and holiness
reveals to us how tarnished and imperfect our own lives are;
yet in Jesus Christ you have shown your unbounded love for us.

So, dazzled by your glory,
marvelling that you love us,
we come to worship you.
All praise and honour and glory be given to you,
eternal God, Father almighty,
through Jesus Christ our Lord. *Amen.*

Confession

We confess to you, Father, that we have sinned.

You have shown us in Jesus that it is better to give than to receive;
   but we have remained selfish and acquisitive.
You have shown us in Jesus that love is stronger than hatred;
   but we have nursed grievances and resentments.
You have shown us in Jesus a new way of living;
   but we have preferred to conform to the standards of the world.
You have shown us in Jesus that the way to true greatness is the
     way of the Cross;
   but we have been afraid to follow in our Master's steps.

And so we have failed ourselves; we have failed others;
and worst of all, we have failed you.

Your will for everyone is wholeness of life,
but by our folly and disobedience
we have prevented ourselves and other people from experiencing
   it.

Forgive us, Father.
Assure us of your mercy and compassion;
enable us to start again;
and grant that by your Spirit's power
we may yet attain to that fullness of life
which you offer to us in Jesus Christ our Lord;
for his sake. *Amen.*

Thanksgiving and Dedication

Almighty God, creator of the universe, we offer you our heartfelt
thanks for the beauty and goodness of your creation and for the
redemption brought to us through Jesus Christ your Son. We
thank you that he had a human birth like ours; that, like us, he
grew through childhood, developing in body, mind and spirit to
become a mature adult. We thank you that he fully shared our
human life and experienced our human death, that as he took our
nature upon him, so we too may participate in his glorious
resurrection.

Especially today we give you thanks for the love and care which
Jesus showed to all who were sick, and for his concern that all
should know the wholeness of life that is your will for everyone.
We thank you too for those whose lives are dedicated to the care
of the sick and the dying, and to the eradication of disease –
doctors, surgeons, nurses, hospital workers, medical researchers
and scientists.

Father, we too would share in the reconciling and healing work of
your Son. To this end we pledge ourselves to your service and to
the service of our community. Help us to be agents of your healing
peace and mediators of your reconciling love; through Jesus Christ
our Lord. *Amen.*

Seventh Sunday before Easter

Adoration

Eternal God, the vast created universe declares your glory;
the hosts of heaven worship your majesty;
the whole earth exalts your holy Name.

We, your people, pause in the midst of life's bustle;
we are still and know you to be God;
we worship and adore you that we may declare your glory;
through Jesus Christ our Lord. *Amen.*

Confession

Loving God,
we read of your mighty acts among your people,
we rejoice in your power displayed in Jesus.

We confess our faithlessness and lack of trust.
We have lived as though your power belonged to the past;
we have not trusted Jesus to work miracles of healing and
    forgiveness in us;
we have been content to live as we have always lived;
we have not opened ourselves to your cleansing and renewing
    grace;
we have looked at our own sin, and been frightened by it;
we have looked at the sin of others, and it has made us smug.

Loving God, forgive us.
Show us the ways in which Jesus can work in us;
show us the power of Jesus to transform human life.
May your loving, healing strength be at work in us,
making forgiveness real,
mending the lives broken by sin.

We ask this confidently, through Jesus Christ your Son, our
    Saviour. *Amen.*

Thanksgiving and Dedication

Thank you, Father, for your glory displayed in the world
and for all your wonderful works.
Thank you for the daily miracles of sight and hearing
by which we know and rejoice in your creating power.
Thank you for your continual renewal of the earth,
for your constant activity in the processes of life.

Thank you, Father, for your glory displayed in Jesus.
Thank you for the miracle of love offered to the undeserving,
of grace at work in human life.
Thank you for his humble birth,
for the power of love revealed in his living and his dying,
in his resurrection and his ascension,
in the coming of his holy and life-giving Spirit.

Thank you, Father, for the faith and fellowship of your holy
    Church.
Thank you for lives made new by the preaching of the Gospel,
for the reconciliation between people of differing outlooks and
    temperaments.
Thank you for the means of grace and for the hope of glory.

Grant that we may live each day in the power of Jesus;
open our lives to the work of your Holy Spirit;
enable us to give ourselves with renewed vision and energy to the
    tasks you have appointed for us.
In Christ you have fed us with the bread of life;
help us to share with others what we have found:
in the Name of Jesus Christ our Lord. *Amen.*

Ash Wednesday

Adoration

Heaven and earth are full of your glory,
almighty, eternal, most holy God.
You deserve the praise of every creature,
you are worthy of worship and honour and love.

Creator, sustainer, redeemer, renewer,
perfect in wisdom and might,
you reign supreme beyond time and space,
in beauty and splendour and light.

We adore you, our God;
we praise your great Name;
we offer you our worship;
through Jesus Christ our Lord. *Amen.*

Confession

God have mercy on us, sinners that we are,
and members of a sinful race.

You created us to love and to serve you,
    but we have been selfish and disobedient.
You have spoken to us again and again through preachers and
        prophets,
    but we have ignored their message.
You sent your Son to be the Saviour of the world,
    but we rejected and crucified him.
You gave us your Holy Spirit to be our guide,
    but we have not listened to his promptings.
You have called us to be members of a royal priesthood,
    but our worship has been cold and half-hearted.
You have given us opportunities to grow in knowledge and love,
    but we have neglected the means of grace.

You have challenged us to live by your Gospel,
   but we have not practised what we preached.

(Silence)

Lord, have mercy.
Christ, have mercy.
Lord, have mercy. *Amen.*

Our sin is great and grievous.
Yet God's mercy and grace are greater.
Hear then Christ's word of love: Your sins are forgiven.
Amen. Thanks be to God.

Thanksgiving and Dedication

God our Father, we thank you for creating the universe
and for sending your Son to be our Saviour.
We thank you for the record of your undeserved love for the
   world,
displayed in Christ's life and death and resurrection and ascension,
and in the gift of the Holy Spirit, our advocate and guide.

Especially at this time we thank you
for the challenge which Christ continues to present
to our conceit and complacency,
our dishonesty and selfishness.
We thank you that he always spoke the truth,
that he strove for the good of all,
and that he was obedient to your will,
though obedience led him to the Cross.
We thank you that through your holy Church
you have given us this solemn season of Lent
as a time when we can examine our lives
and measure them against the standard of Christ.

God our Father, we are yours,
created and redeemed by your love.
We dedicate ourselves again to you,
praying that you will show us, by the Spirit of truth,
the depth of our inbred sin;
that you will help us, by the Spirit of wisdom,
to be honest in our estimate of ourselves;

that you will enable us, by the Spirit of power,
to live more nearly as we pray;
and that you will bring us at last, by the Spirit of life,
to the peace and joy of your kingdom;
for the sake of Jesus Christ our Lord. *Amen.*

Sixth Sunday before Easter (Lent 1)

Adoration

Lord God, King of the universe, ruler of all time and space,
you alone are worthy of all the praise
of every person in every age.
You dwell in glory beyond our imagining, in light unapproachable,
yet you come to us in Jesus.
We praise you for that mystery of your grace, wonder of wonders!

Lord Jesus Christ, sharing our humanity,
bone of our bone and flesh of our flesh,
to you belongs all the praise imaginable:
  mild you laid your glory by;
  a helpless baby in his mother's arms;
  our God contracted to a span;
  taking the form of a servant;
  ready for God's calling to ministry;
  sharing baptism with repentant sinners;
  spending yourself for all who needed you;
  risking the envy of powerful men;
  giving your life a ransom for many;
  tested and tortured;
  tempted as we are, yet without sin;
  obedient to death, even the death of the Cross.

Holy Spirit, leading us into all the truth that is in Jesus,
to you belongs all the praise imaginable.
Through you our lives become a home for the Christ.
Wonder of wonders!

We are lost in wonder, love and praise. *Amen.*

Sixth Sunday before Easter

Confession

Lord, we sinners confess to you what we are.

We like the path of life to be easy, comfortable, untroubled.
We like problems to melt away, hardships to be smoothed over,
    stones to turn into bread for us.
We do not want the hard way that Jesus takes.

We like every step to be free from fears.
We like to see mighty power helping us at every turn.
We like miracles to be happening for our benefit.
We do not want the faithful way that Jesus takes.

We like the world to be at our feet,
to be lords over our lives, and everyone else's,
to be kings of creation, viewing everything from a great height.
We do not want the humble way that Jesus takes.

Lord, by all the grace of those forty desert days,
arm us against those temptations,
alert us to their corruption,
forgive us our sins.
Teach us to tread the way that Jesus takes;
for his sake. *Amen.*

Thanksgiving and Dedication

We thank you, Lord God of all eternity,
that you have not left us to struggle with our sins on our own.
You have acted so decisively for us in Jesus our Saviour.

We thank you, Jesus Christ our Lord.
    When we are too hurt to forgive others,
        you are overflowing with mercy to all;
    when we are too callous to notice the pain of others,
        you feel it in yourself;
    when life bewilders us and we do not know what the good is,
        you keep hold of God's righteous will;
    when we are at our weakest, in pain or doubt or distress or self-
        pity,
        you know our frailty but remain strong for us;
    when we want to run away from life,
        you keep with us and hold resolutely to God's loving purpose.

We thank you, Holy Spirit,
through whom the grace which was in Christ
lives now within us.

Lord and Saviour, now we commit ourselves to
   your readiness in forgiving,
   your sensitivity to others,
   your grasp of God's will,
   your strength despite weakness,
   your resolution in God's way;

in the power of the Spirit. *Amen.*

Fifth Sunday before Easter (Lent 2)

Adoration

Everlasting God, you hold all things in your hands:
time, space, and all creation.
We realize how small we are,
and yet we rejoice that through your Spirit
we are enabled to respond to your goodness.
The wonder of your suffering love,
revealed to us in your Son Jesus Christ,
is almost too much for us to bear,
and beyond our expression in word or thought.
Accept, we pray, the unspoken adoration
that comes from our thankful hearts;
for the sake of our Saviour, Jesus Christ. *Amen.*

Confession

Loving Father, we are so readily tempted,
so fearful, so prone to lose our courage.
Sometimes we take the easy way out,
allowing evil to triumph,
shrinking from action,
because we do not hold firmly to our true beliefs.
We complain about our own suffering,
which is as nothing
in comparison with that of your Son, our Saviour.

Forgive us, Father,
that it is our own waywardness, our own blindness,
that prevents us from recognizing you in every part of our lives.
Forgive us that we too often expect to find all the answers
or to see the way ahead.
May we be more ready to learn from our Lord Jesus Christ
the way of trust in your fatherly care.
We ask it in his Name. *Amen.*

Thanksgiving and Dedication

Almighty God, you are worthy of all thanks and praise.
You made the world we inhabit;
you made men and women in your own image;
you redeemed us by your love.
In our Saviour Jesus Christ
you have fought the decisive battle against evil;
for he who was born on earth for our salvation,
who lived among us and died on the Cross,
is risen from the dead and alive for evermore,
the victor over evil, sin and death.

And so we thank you, Father,
for the redemption of the world
by the sufferings and the victory of your Son Jesus Christ.
We thank you too for all who have suffered for your sake in times
    past;
for those who are suffering now;
and for all who have given their lives
for love of you and of their fellow men and women.

As we think of the steadfastness of Jesus,
we pray that we shall be more ready to dedicate our lives to you.
We would be true disciples,
ever seeking to learn more of you and your will for us.
We want to show by the way we live
that your kingdom is a present reality,
not merely a pious hope beyond time and space.
In deep thankfulness for the life and death and resurrection of
    your Son,
we offer ourselves to you in his Name. *Amen.*

Fourth Sunday before Easter (Lent 3)

Adoration

Glorious King of heaven,
with angels and archangels and all the company of heaven
   we worship and adore you.

Eternal King of kings,
with all your people who dwell on earth
   we bow in homage at your feet.

Almighty King of all creation,
with all your wonderful works
   we bless and praise your holy Name.

Immortal King of love and Shepherd of our souls,
Lord Jesus who was born for us,
and died for us,
we humbly offer the songs of our lips,
   the work of our hands,
   the service of our lives
   the love of our hearts,
     to your praise and glory. *Amen.*

Confession

We confess, Lord,

that in our obsession with earthly things and worldly standards
we forget you and your kingdom;

we take the gifts of creation for granted;
we abuse and pollute them;
we use them for our own selfish ends;

by our wilfulness, perversity, and folly
we have grieved your heart of love
and added to the sufferings of the world.

72

Yet we come to you in penitence and in faith,
knowing that you will heal, restore, and forgive;
in the Name of Jesus Christ our Lord. *Amen.*

Thanksgiving and Dedication

We thank you, Father, for the joy of living in your lovely world,
for the love of family and friends and the sense of belonging to a
    community,
for the privilege of being members of your Church
and for your call to service.

We thank you even more that in those wilderness experiences
when the world is hostile,
when those nearest to us let us down,
when our fellow-Christians misunderstand,
and when we become uncertain of our calling,
your Son, our Lord Jesus Christ, who has experienced and
    overcome all these things, is with us.

With awe and wonder
we recall the cost of our redemption,
when Jesus died on the Cross that we might have Life.
We humbly pray that, prompted by the Spirit,
we may be ready to take up our Cross and follow Jesus
and that, sharing in his sufferings,
we may experience the power of his resurrection;
we ask it in his Name and for his sake. *Amen.*

Third Sunday before Easter (Lent 4)

Adoration

Eternal God, we praise you,
for you are the source of light and life.

Your word made the whole of creation,
in all its beauty and splendour, *[handwritten: variety]*
bringing order out of chaos, *[handwritten: all its variety + detail]*
light out of darkness.
We praise you that the evidence of your creative activity
is all around us still. *[handwritten: for life + growth in a million gardens + fields]*

We praise you, Father,
for your supreme revelation of yourself
in our Lord Jesus Christ,
and for the clear vision of your love
that we see in him.

Inspire us now with the life and light he came to bring,
that our praises may be worthy of him
and resound to his honour and glory; *[handwritten: Make this time of Lent a time of new devotion + love]*
for his sake. *Amen.*

Confession

Father, you know us better than we know ourselves,
and in the light of your glory *[handwritten: goodness]*
all the darkness of our sin is revealed.

In your presence we confess
  our failure to respond fully to your commandment to love,
  our reluctance to follow you,
  our desire to please ourselves rather than to serve you.

We confess
    that we have only feebly responded to that clear revelation,
    given to us in Jesus,
    and that we have allowed the light of his glory
    to be obscured by our own apathy and indifference.

Father, you know us better than we know ourselves;
but we know that we are sinners.
Grant us an awareness of sins forgiven
and your abundant grace;
through Jesus Christ our Lord. *Amen.*

Thanksgiving and Dedication

Father, we thank you for those glimpses we have had of your
glory, which have brought us to our knees in wonder and praise.
We thank you for the quiet moments, when we have been
surrounded by the beauty of nature in the valleys, on the hills, or
by the water. We thank you for the stirring moments, when music
or drama has lifted us beyond the ordinary to new realms of bliss
and delight.

We thank you for those moments of insight and vision of Jesus, the
living Word, which have come to us in fellowship with other
Christians, as we have shared an act of worship, or quietly read
your word in our homes. We thank you for the coming of Jesus
into the world, for his life and death, his resurrection and
ascension, the light shining in our darkness, bringing divine
illumination, renewing our vision.

We thank you for those who seek to widen and enrich our vision
through their work as artists, musicians, theologians, teachers or
preachers. We thank you for the way these insights can transform
our everyday life and experience, bringing new hope and fresh
inspiration.

Father, we offer ourselves again to you, rejoicing that we have
seen your glory in the face of your Son, committed, in the power of
the Spirit, to share our vision with others; in the Name of Jesus
Christ our Lord. *Amen.*

Second Sunday before Easter (Passion Sunday)

Adoration

God our Father, we worship and adore you;

you are all majesty and all might, unimaginably great,
alone in power and strength.

you have fought against evil and crushed it;
yet you have also redeemed us in love and in pity,
and cared for us all the days of our life.

Above all, you have sent your Son Jesus Christ
for the salvation of mankind;

all earthly powers and authorities were overcome by him;
he triumphed over them in his glorious majesty.

Through him let us put off our corruption and wickedness;
let us rise with him to new life,
through faith in your power and your glory,
to whom be praise for ever and ever. *Amen.*

Confession

God our Father, we confess before you our own ingratitude and
   wickedness.
When we should have been thankful, we have forgotten you;
when we should have worked for you, we have given our energies
   to our own concerns.
We have neglected our duty as children of God:
we have been lukewarm in our worship,
fainthearted in our prayers,
and lazy in the study of your word.
Help us, Lord, to change our sinful natures
and be born again to a new life of service and dedication to you.

May we be rooted in Christ,
built up in him,
and established through him in the faith;
through him who took our sins and nailed them to his Cross –
Jesus Christ our Lord. *Amen.*

Thanksgiving and Dedication

Almighty God, we give thanks for all your blessings, and
especially at this time for the life on earth of your Son Jesus Christ,
who refused to avoid his destiny but chose to endure the Cross,
and to glorify his Father in heaven. We give thanks for the truth of
the great paradox that he who loves his life shall lose it, but
whoever loses his life for Christ's sake shall find it. Take us to be
your servants, Lord, and help us to know this truth in our lives.
May we follow the example of him who was lifted up on the Cross,
who was raised from the dead, and who is exalted to your right
hand in glory. Make us steadfast in your service, Lord, and may
our own lives be an example to others of your love for everyone.
We ask it through him who set his face towards Calvary – Jesus
Christ our Lord. *Amen.*

The Sunday before Easter (Palm Sunday)

Adoration

Lord God of mystery which we cannot fathom,
we honour your Name.
Eternally the same in love and in purpose,
yet your nature seems contradictory to our changing human
    nature.
We open ourselves to you, seeking to understand.

Heavenly King, placed high above the firmament,
but lowly and riding on an ass,
we want to follow you.

Lord Jesus, who entered Jerusalem once in public and in triumph,
you continually come quietly to the open heart,
so we adore you in silence, and want to receive you.

(Silence)

Jesus Christ, exalted and lifted up in heaven,
and on the Cross,
we acclaim you.

Man of Sorrows, disfigured yet glorious,
harshly treated yet patiently enduring,
we worship you.

Lamb of God, the full, perfect and sufficient sacrifice for our sins,
we offer you our praise. *Amen.*

Confession

Forgive us, Father, for the times when, like lost sheep, we have
    strayed from your path, confident that we knew the way. Pardon
    us that in pride and wilfulness we have wanted preferential
    treatment at the expense of others.

When we try to get our own way by harsh words, by anger, or by
bullying, teach us the meekness which patiently endures, whose
anger is controlled and exercised on behalf of the oppressed.
When we are tempted to do nothing in the face of clear human
need, because action will be costly or difficult, set before us the
example of Jesus.

We confess that we are tempted to leave your path because we are
afraid of the cost of the journey. At these times, Lord, you
gather us in; you show us the way; you equip us with the means
to reach our goal; and you invite our obedient response to your
offer.

Give us the faith to make the journey; and, if the Cross seems to
lie ahead, help us to see further than its apparent failure to the
victory that Christ won there and to the eternal life that lies
beyond.

We ask it in our Saviour's Name. *Amen.*

Thanksgiving and Dedication

Heavenly Father,
we thank you for your love in creating the world
and in sending Jesus to make plain your intentions for us.
We thank you that when he faced opposition
he did not use force;
we recognize through his example
the strength of gentleness and the weakness of power;
we see in his death and resurrection
the victory of unselfish love.

And so we offer thanks
  for those who seek to bring about justice and harmony between
    those in conflict;
  for the United Nations and for everything that promotes
    understanding among the nations;
  for agencies of conciliation between conflicting factions;
    and for those who help others who are going through hard
      times
    to find fulfilment of their needs.

The Sunday before Easter

We thank you that, through the Holy Spirit,
we can gain a broad vision of society
as your love would have it,
where no one need be in want or fear;
and that we can pursue this vision with determination
but with an awareness of problems and constraints.

We remember, Father,
that Jesus was not made afraid by opposition;
that he set his face steadfastly towards Jerusalem
and entered the city in triumph.
We pray that we also may act bravely
and commit ourselves to your will
that through us your persuasive love may be demonstrated
and victories gained;
for the sake of Jesus Christ our Lord. *Amen.*

Thursday before Easter (Maundy Thursday)

Adoration

Great God,
you astonish us by your closeness.
Creator and keeper of all that is,
you give yourself to the humblest of your creation.
Ruler of all,
you choose a people for yourself
and guide and care for them
in good times and bad;
and when they turn from you
you call them all to follow your Son.
He came as a servant, not as a master,
and gave himself to buy freedom for many.

We bless you, our seeking, saving God,
for this sign of your love,
for this token of your longing.
Such things are beyond our invention or imagining,
but you have touched us and healed us
in him who was wounded for our transgressions,
and bruised for our iniquities,
whose chastisement has made us whole.

God beyond our understanding,
God, made known within our suffering,
God, redeeming us in our sinfulness,
we worship you;
in Jesus Christ our Lord. *Amen.*

Confession

Father,
we recall that Jesus washed his disciples' feet
and set us an example.

Thursday before Easter

We find it hard to serve others.
We forget our Lord
and lord it over others,
letting them serve us.
We ignore our Teacher,
and choose our own examples,
suiting ourselves.
We turn Good News into counsels of despair.

Restore in us the image of your Son.
Recall to us the spirit that was in Christ.
Remove from us all selfishness
and desire to control others;
and let Christ rule in us,
let Christ make us clean,
let Christ, the servant of all,
forgive us and make us
parables of his love;
for his Name's sake. *Amen.*

Thanksgiving and Dedication

We bless you, Lord our God, ruler of the universe,
for you create the world.
All things depend on you for life:
everything is filled with your goodness:
all that we see and touch and hear,
all that we taste and smell.
How good it all is!
How good you are!

In Egypt your people ate the bitter bread of slavery.
In the desert you gave them fresh water
and manna for their daily bread.
You led them to a land of milk and honey.

The night before he suffered,
Jesus blessed you for bread
and raised the cup of salvation.
On the Cross he made a new covenant
and sealed the promise of your love for ever.

We praise you, Lord God,
for that which was from the beginning,
which we have heard and seen
and touched with our hands,
the bread of life which we have tasted
and share with others.
Join us to the fellowship of those who recognize you,
and give us to those who need you;
for the sake of him who gave himself for all mankind,
Jesus Christ our Lord. *Amen.*

Good Friday

Adoration

Almighty and ever-present God, we worship you for what you are,
and rejoice in the knowledge we have of you.
We recall with awe and wonder
your power in creation, your wisdom, holiness, and majesty.
We praise you that you have revealed yourself to us,
and above all that we see you in Jesus Christ,
the eternal Word, yet one of us.
We praise you that in him we see our eternal God,
stooping, living, loving, and dying,
that we might live.

Almighty and ever-present God, we worship and adore you,
in the Name of Jesus Christ our Lord. *Amen.*

Confession

Loving Father, we remember today
all that you have wrought for us in Jesus Christ.

We recall his sacrifice upon the Cross
and confess with wonder that it was our God who died on Calvary.

We can neither earn nor deserve all that was done for us that day.
We can but recall, search ourselves, and offer ourselves in
     penitence and faith.

We ask your forgiveness now,
that the judgment we deserve
may be tempered by the grace and self-giving of Calvary,
by your love, ceaseless, unexhausted, unmerited, and free;
through the merits of Jesus Christ our Saviour. *Amen.*

Thanksgiving and Dedication

Gracious heavenly Father, we thank you for all the signs we have
of your concern for us.
We thank you for revealing yourself in so many ways,
and especially that you showed yourself,
clearly and for ever, in Jesus Christ.

We thank you for his coming, his ministry, his words, and his
    example.
Today we praise you that he did not hold back from death itself,
the death which we die,
and that through death he brought us life.
We thank you for that victory of love.

We cannot match his giving,
but what we are we give to you,
confident that your Spirit can breathe new life and power into us.
Take us and use us, that something of Christ's loving and giving,
his living and dying, may be seen in us;
for his sake. *Amen.*

Easter Day
(1st set)

Adoration

Eternal God, our heavenly Father,
with gladness in our hearts and songs on our lips
we come into your house this Easter Day
to worship you and to celebrate your mightiest act –
the raising of Jesus Christ from the dead.

Lord Jesus Christ,
we rejoice that death could not hold you in its grip,
but that you rose again triumphant,
greeting your incredulous friends,
convincing them that you were the same Jesus
who was dead but is alive for evermore;
changing their sorrow to joy,
giving them new life and new hope.

We too are your friends.
Reveal yourself to us now in your risen power, we pray,
as we worship and adore you;
for your Name's sake. *Amen.*

so that we today may confess you to be Lord

Confession

Forgive us, Lord Jesus,
that, like your friends of old,
we are often subject to fears and doubts,
lack of faith,
and limited awareness. *so that your teaching is achieved*

Grant us the gift of the Holy Spirit,
that he may reveal to us your truth,
so that our fears may be overcome,
our doubts resolved,

86

our faith quickened,
and our awareness deepened.
For your Name's sake we ask it. *Amen.*

Thanksgiving and Dedication

Almighty God, creator of all things,
we thank you for the spring of the year –
    earth released from the icy grip of winter;
    the green blade of wheat rising through the dark earth;
    flowers in hedgerow and garden;
    trees in bud, blossom ready to break;
    fledglings in the nest, lambs in the field –
    everywhere the promise of new life.

We thank you for the gift of your Son, our Saviour Jesus Christ,
    who became man,
    lived a life of love and service,
    and died for us on the Cross.·
We thank you that it was in a garden in springtime that he rose
    again,
    Lord of life and Conqueror of death.

We thank you for the gift of the Holy Spirit
    who brings us into new life in Christ.
We dedicate ourselves again to you,
    praying that, in the power of your Spirit,
    we may be strengthened to serve you in the Church and in the
        world,
for the sake of Jesus Christ, our risen Lord. *Amen.*

Easter Day
(2nd set)

Adoration

Christ is risen!
Mighty God, we have no words that can express your power and
    our awe.
Christ is risen!
You raised him from the dead.
Blessing and honour and glory and power be yours, almighty God,
    for ever and ever.
Christ is risen!
You raised him from the dead.
All creation sings the glory of the risen and victorious Son.
Christ is risen!
You raised him from the dead.
We are free from the power of sin and death.
Praise be to you, the God and Father of our Lord Jesus Christ.
Mighty God, we have no words that can express your power and
    our awe.
But with adoring hearts we now affirm:
Christ is risen!
He is risen indeed! Alleluia! *Amen.*

Confession

For every time we have allowed despair to take possession of us,
forgive us, Lord.
For every time we have permitted the power of sin to master our
    lives,
forgive us, Lord.
For our lack of trust in you,
forgive us, Lord.
For our fear of death and of the unknown,
forgive us, Lord.

Re-assure us of your transforming and forgiving love.
May the joy of this triumphant day reach deep down into our
   personalities,
making us anew in your image, helping us to share in the victory of
   Christ.
We ask this for his sake. *Amen.*

Thanksgiving and Dedication

Loving Father, we give you thanks and praise. You love the world
so much that you did not leave us in darkness, but sent us Jesus
your Son. We praise you because his story did not end with death
on the Cross. You brought him back from death with power and
glory, and we your people praise you for the hope this brings us.

Lord Jesus Christ, we give you thanks and praise. You have taken
on yourself all the world's sin and shame. You have overcome the
power of evil for us, and we your people praise you for our share in
your victory.

Holy Spirit of God, we give you thanks and praise. You make the
victory of Jesus real to us. You work in us, you make us alive in
Christ, and we your people praise you for what you do for us day
by day.

Help us, wonderful God, not to praise you with words alone, but
to give ourselves anew to our Christian calling. May the light and
victory which we celebrate today so fill our lives that we may be
faithful in and through all things; through Jesus Christ, our risen
Lord. *Amen.*

89

The Sunday after Easter
(Year 1)

*its design, & its
awesonly
... ... G*

Adoration

Lord God, we adore you; you are a God of power:
  the whole universe is alive with your energy;
  of its potential, immensity and complexity we know only a little,
  but it points us to you as its creator and sustainer.

Lord God, we adore you; you are also a God of love:
  your power has a purpose,
  and we see evidence of that in the beauty of creation,
  and in the human potential for understanding and creativity.

Above all, your love and your power
  are focused in the life and death and rising again of Jesus of
    Nazareth.

With joy we celebrate his resurrection,
  by which you have shown yourself to be a God of power,
  stronger than all the powers of darkness and sin,
  keeping us safe in your care;
  but you have shown yourself also to be a God of love,
  love that was not quenched by the hatred and bitterness of the
    Cross;
  and because of this we believe that you will go on loving us
  until the end of time.

Lord God, we adore you – the God of power and the God of love;
in the Name of Jesus Christ our Lord. *Amen.*

Confession

Lord God, you made the hearts of the disciples glad
with the knowledge of the resurrection of Jesus, your Son;

90

forgive us because, like them, we find the truth of Easter so hard
    to believe;
forgive us that we are so easily downcast, and given to despair;
forgive us that, although we claim to live by the resurrection faith,
we so often appear to believe that suffering is simply a tragedy and
    that death is the end;
forgive us that we take so much convincing of the hope that you
    give to the world.

(Silence)

Come to us, Lord God, in the power of the risen Christ.
Take away our crippling doubts and fears,
and through your Holy Spirit bring us to life in your service;
for the sake of Jesus Christ our Lord. *Amen.*

Thanksgiving and Dedication

God and Father of our Lord Jesus Christ,
we praise you because in your great mercy
we have been born anew to a living hope
through the resurrection of Jesus Christ from the dead.

You created us, and all things,
and gave us a place within your purpose.
When, in our ignorance and disobedience, we turned against you,
you sent your Son, Jesus, to be our Saviour.

We thank you that he became man,
and shared fully in our human life;
we thank you that, in obedience to your will,
he suffered the loneliness and agony of death on the Cross for us;
we thank you that he has risen again to reign with you in glory.

We thank you that by his death he has conquered death
and that by his resurrection he has opened the way
to the freedom and peace of heaven.

Send us your Holy Spirit, Father,
that, in power and confidence, we may live as his disciples,
and serve him in the world,
until with all his people we come at last
to the love and joy and peace of your kingdom;
we ask it for Christ's sake. *Amen.*

The Sunday after Easter
(Year 2)

Adoration

Holy God, our Father, you are the source of all life
and it is sustained by your will alone.
When the Israelites wandered in the desert,
you provided manna to sustain them.
You fed them on their journey with bread from heaven
and saved them from desolation and despair.
When our spirits fail, and the meaning of life eludes us,
and we appear to wander in circles,
we too may be sustained and cheered by living bread,
food of angels, token of immortality.
The body and blood of Christ
is food and drink for our hungry, parched souls.
Through these gifts you bless us with renewed courage
to continue in your love.
Your care is never removed from us through life or death.
Nothing on earth is able to separate us from your love.
Glory be to you, our Father,
through Jesus Christ our risen Lord. *Amen.*

Confession

We confess to you, almighty God,
that we are sinners who are guilty of defying the law of love.
In public and in private
we have abused or neglected the love which sets others before self.
We have failed to promote the interests of your love
above and beyond our own temporary satisfactions.
Life seems too short to make amends, and death looms
    threateningly.

We ask to be forgiven,
granted time and opportunity to repair our lives,
and, above all, enabled to know the gift of your love and
    acceptance in our hearts.
As we receive this assurance,
may the sting of guilt and the fear of death be removed.
May we who are guilty be acquitted by your love;
through the power of the risen Christ.
We ask it for his sake. *Amen.*

Thanksgiving and Dedication

Father, we offer you thanks through Christ
for the abating of our souls' hunger,
the quenching of our spirits' thirst,
and the lasting satisfaction which Christ alone can give.

Whenever we turn back to him,
dissatisfied with rival remedies for restlessness,
he is always ready to receive us.

Father, we are grateful for the peace you give us through Christ.
Our wills are confused, but you have only one will –
to give eternal life to those who look to Jesus.
We thank you for your great condescension
in stooping down to us through Christ's coming, living and dying,
that we may be raised up by his resurrection.

As we offer ourselves to you again in gratitude,
we ask that we may be enabled by your Spirit
to celebrate the resurrection by sharing our bread with the hungry,
receiving others as brothers and sisters in Christ,
listening to discover your will for us,
and being bold to do it;
through Jesus Christ our Saviour. *Amen.*

Second Sunday after Easter
(Year 1)

Adoration

Eternal Father God,
holy beyond our sense of purity,
mighty beyond our sense of power,
merciful beyond our sense of compassion,
we adore you.
We glimpse your greatness
and are amazed that you care for us,
selfish, rebellious creatures.
In Jesus Christ we realize the true extent
of your love for us and involvement with us,
and our hearts are full of gratitude.
Our response to you is inadequate,
yet we respond as we can:
all praise and glory be given to you, now and for ever. *Amen.*

Confession

Father, only you know how much we need forgiveness,
and only you can forgive us.
We humbly confess our failures to you,
confident of your forgiving nature:
    our failure to recognize your speaking to us
      through your Son, your Church, your word and your world;
      our failure to live in the power of the risen Christ;
      our renunciation of good and our compromise with evil.
Grant us freedom from the past,
resolve in the present,
and dedication in the future,
that we may be better disciples of Jesus Christ your Son;
for his sake. *Amen.*

Thanksgiving and Dedication

We give thanks to you, our Father,
for your creative power
and your constant care for your creation.

We give thanks to you, our Father,
for the way, the truth, and the life you have revealed to us
in Jesus Christ your Son;
for the power of his death and resurrection;
for the times when we have looked back in wonder
and seen your hand guiding our lives,
your word directing our ways,
and your nearness warming our hearts;
for the occasions when we have glimpsed more of your truth
and experienced your presence
in the breaking of the bread.

We give thanks to you, our Father,
for the gift of the Holy Spirit,
who reveals to us the things of Jesus
and leads us into all truth.

We present ourselves to you, humbly and thankfully.
Make us into disciples who bring glory to your Name;
for the sake of Jesus Christ our Lord. *Amen.*

Second Sunday after Easter
(Year 2)

Adoration

Almighty Father, the source of all beauty and goodness and love,
we come together to worship you.
We are tiny people set in your vast and wonderful universe,
too much absorbed by the transitory things of life.
But today in this holy place we turn to you,
to your eternity and greatness.
Widen our horizons, deepen our experience,
and carry us out of ourselves;
for in you alone is found joy and peace and salvation;
through Jesus Christ our Lord. *Amen.*

Confession

God our Father, help us to live in love and charity with others,
and, as we ask for your forgiveness, enable us to be forgiving.
Take from our lives the hidden grudges and concealed hate.
Forgive us that we have so often denied you;
that like lost sheep we have turned away from you;
that we have sung with our lips
what we have not had the courage to practise in our lives.

Father, forgive our sins, comfort our sorrows,
calm our fears, and take from us every proud thought.
So fill us with love and concern for others,
and make us ready to help and quick to forgive;
we ask this through Jesus Christ our Saviour. *Amen.*

Thanksgiving and Dedication

Loving heavenly Father,
we thank you for every good thing in our lives;
for home and friends and family;
for all the beauty and loveliness in the world about us,
which has lifted our hearts and made us glad;
for life itself with all its promise and possibility.

We thank you that in every great experience of life,
when it seemed as if we were passing through water and fire,
we were not alone, but you were there as Saviour and Friend.

We thank you that we are yours, created for your glory;
that you have called us all by name;
that through Jesus Christ, the great Shepherd of the sheep,
who lived and died and rose again for us,
you have redeemed us;
and that your love will never finally let us go,
or ultimately give us up.

We thank you that so often you have come to us
in the ordinary and everyday things of life,
in our work and in our leisure.
Help us there to seek you and find you and serve you,
as in Christ you have sought and found and served us.
We ask it for his sake. *Amen.*

Third Sunday after Easter
(Year 1)

Adoration

Lord God, our heavenly Father,
we praise you for the Good News
you have proclaimed to all nations
through the life, death and resurrection of your Son,
Jesus Christ our Lord.
In him the humble poor are exalted;
he binds up the wounds of the broken-hearted,
and sets the captives free.
We praise you for his resurrection,
and for the living presence of his Spirit in our midst today.

May we celebrate the joy of that presence,
and the transforming power of the Good News Christ offers to all,
as we bring you our worship and praise;
for his Name's sake. *Amen.*

Confession

Lord Jesus, you have commanded your Church to feed your
    sheep,
and yet millions of our brothers and sisters are hungry,
and our own society is spiritually impoverished.

You came to bring Good News to the poor,
but we still measure human beings by their wealth and the number
    of their possessions.

You came to set the captives free,
and yet, all over the world,
men and women who stand up for their beliefs
are in prison, with little hope of release.

You came to give sight to the blind,
yet we who hear your Name
still wilfully shut our eyes to the things we have no desire to see.

Risen Lord, we confess to you our blindness,
our selfishness, our apathy,
our faltering witness, and our hesitating service.

Grant us this day your forgiveness and your love,
that we may live your risen life
and truly care for your sheep,
until that day when the whole earth shall call you Lord
and praise your holy Name. *Amen.*

Thanksgiving and Dedication

Father God,
since the dawn of time you have held the universe in being.
When time is no more, you will still be Lord of all.
In the Name of Jesus Christ,
we thank you, heavenly Father.

We thank you that you have sent your Son
to preach the Good News of your kingdom to all who have ears to
    hear.
He proclaimed your truth, he showed us your love,
and he taught us your ways.
In the Name of Jesus Christ,
we thank you, heavenly Father.

We thank you that he was crucified for us,
and that he rose from the dead
and walked and talked with his followers and friends.
In the Name of Jesus Christ,
we thank you, heavenly Father.

We thank you that you have given us your Holy Spirit
to comfort us in our affliction
and afflict us in our comfort.
He sets before us the vision of your kingdom,
and day by day his power sustains us.
In the Name of Jesus Christ,
we thank you, heavenly Father.

Third Sunday after Easter

Send us out, Father,
in the power of the risen Christ,
to live and work each day to your praise and glory;
for the sake of Jesus Christ our Lord. *Amen.*

Third Sunday after Easter
(Year 2)

Adoration

Eternal God, holy and majestic, glorious and almighty,
your power and your purity leave us breathless.
We adore you, the source of all goodness,
the creator of all life.
How great is our amazement
that you should care for us, your rebel creatures;
that you should act again and again
within the events of our human history
to bring us salvation;
and that, in Christ, you should give yourself to the uttermost for
    us.
How great is our wonder
as we contemplate your self-giving love
displayed upon the Cross of Christ
and your almighty power
revealed in his resurrection from the dead.
How great you are, our Lord, our God!
May all praise and honour be given to you, Father almighty,
now and for ever. *Amen.*

Confession

Gracious God, we confess to you what we are –
sinners in need of forgiveness.
You have called us to die to sin
and to be raised to new life with Christ,
but we have been reluctant to leave the old life behind.
We have been content to compromise with evil,
satisfied with our worldly lives,
unwilling to be changed by your love,

afraid to sacrifice our security
in order to experience life in all its fullness.
Gracious God, forgive our faint-hearted response to your
    goodness.
Forgive our complacency and self-satisfaction.
Challenge us again to discard our old nature
and to put on the new,
which is constantly being renewed in the image of its creator.
We ask it in the Name of Jesus Christ,
our risen, living, reigning Lord. *Amen.*

Thanksgiving and Dedication

Father eternal, we give you thanks
for your creating and redeeming love.

In love you made the universe out of nothing;
in love you created the human race.
In love, after we had fallen into sin,
you brought about a new creation
by giving your Son to be our Saviour.
Through what he taught and by the way he lived
he revealed your loving purposes for us and for everyone.

We thank you that, by his death and mighty resurrection,
he has conquered sin and death for us;
that he lives for ever to intercede for us;
that he is for us the Resurrection and the Life.
We thank you that, by the power of the Spirit,
we are enabled to die to sin and to rise to new life in Christ.

Loving God, Father of us all,
we dedicate ourselves again to you.
Keep us faithful in your service, now and always;
for the sake of Jesus Christ our Lord. *Amen.*

Fourth Sunday after Easter
(Year 1)

Adoration

Blessed be God the Father,
by whose great mercy we have been born again to a living hope
through the resurrection of Jesus Christ from the dead.

Blessed be God the Son,
who died for our sins
and rose again for our justification.

Blessed be God the Holy Spirit,
who bears witness with our spirits.
that we are the children of God.

To you, blessed God, Father, Son, and Holy Spirit,
we ascribe all blessing, honour and glory for ever. *Amen.*

Confession

Lord God, we do not always readily confess our helplessness and
    need;
but you know our works:
you know how often we are lukewarm in your service,
how often we have denied you,
how often we have failed to tend your sheep.
And so now we acknowledge that we are sinners, poor and blind
    and naked.

But you do not leave us forsaken and desolate.
Your Son Jesus Christ stands at the door and knocks;
help us to hear his voice and open the door,
that he may come in to us,
and eat with us, and we with him.
We ask it in his Name. *Amen.*

Fourth Sunday after Easter

Thanksgiving and Dedication

We thank you, God our Father,
for our creation, preservation, and all the blessings of this life.

We thank you for the redemption of the world by our Lord Jesus
     Christ,
for he is the Paschal Lamb who was offered for us
and has taken away the sin of the world.
By his death he has destroyed death,
and by his rising again he has restored to us eternal life.

We thank you for the sanctification of our lives by your Holy Spirit
who brings salvation to us,
so that we may die with Christ and rise with him.

Not as we ought but as we are able
we offer ourselves to you,
and ask you not to weigh our merits
but to remember your mercy.
Strengthen us by your Holy Spirit
to show our love for you by our care for others,
and bring us all at the last to a joyful resurrection;
through Jesus Christ our risen Lord and Saviour. *Amen.*

Fourth Sunday after Easter
(Year 2)

Adoration

Almighty God,
before whose holiness and light
the angels in heaven protect their faces;
accept our songs of praise
as we approach the throne of your heavenly glory;
and grant that as we hear your most holy word
and celebrate the power and presence of your Holy Spirit
we may see the splendour of your majesty
in the face of your Son, our Saviour, Jesus Christ. *Amen.*

Confession

God our Father,
into whose house we have entered
both for the forgiveness of our sins
and the renewal of our lives;
accept our unspoken confession
and the imperfection of our penitence.
We confess to you
that we have abandoned your way,
spurned your truth,
and refused your invitation to fullness of life.
Have mercy on us,
free us from our sins,
and cleanse us from all iniquity;
for the sake of your Son, our Saviour, Jesus Christ. *Amen.*

Fourth Sunday after Easter

Thanksgiving and Dedication

Blessed are you, Lord God, King of all creation;
by your grace you have made us
and in your mercy you have called us to yourself.
We praise you for the faith of the patriarchs
and the voice of the prophets;
we bless you for the gift of your only-begotten Son
and for his obedience to your will.
We praise you for the life-giving mystery of his holy Cross
and for the power of his glorious resurrection;
we bless you for the indwelling of the Holy Spirit
and the fruits of your grace;
we praise you for the witness of your Church
and for the testimony of your saints.
Heavenly Father,
accept us as we offer ourselves to you
in joyful surrender;
and grant that, through the intercession of Christ, our great High
    Priest,
we may walk in the way of your Gospel,
rejoice in its truth,
and embrace for ever the promise of eternal life;
through Jesus Christ our Lord,
who lives and reigns with you and the Holy Spirit,
one God, now and for ever. *Amen.*

Fifth Sunday after Easter

Adoration

We hear the promise of Jesus:
When the Spirit of truth comes, he will guide you into all the truth.

We pray together for the fulfilment of that promise.

Father, we come to you in praise,
for the Heir of your majesty is the friend who shared our
    weakness,
and his rising from the dead has made us heirs with him.
As we gather in him to worship you,
we know that our prayer is heard,
that your Spirit has new truth to quicken us with joy.

Let him declare to us the inward truths of Jesus:
    the words of our Saviour, to echo in our conscience,
    the face of our Saviour, to look into our heart,
    the wounds of our Saviour, to bring us forgiveness,
    the life of our Saviour, to strengthen our service.

In the Name of our Saviour, we come to you in adoration. *Amen*.

Confession

Father, it is more than the wonder of your being,
more than our smallness,
that hides your presence from us;
for we have disobeyed you
and have failed in care for our neighbours.
We have been discontented with you,
dissatisfied with the limits of our life,
quick to demand and slow to trust.

Fifth Sunday after Easter

For the sake of your Son, whom you have made for us the way to
   peace,
renew to us now your pardon, most gracious Lord and Father.
   Amen.

As in Adam all die, even so in Christ shall all be made alive.
Hear then Christ's word of grace to us: Your sins are forgiven.
Amen. Thanks be to God.

Thanksgiving and Dedication

Father, you work with us for good in everything.
   We praise your Name.
You call us to work with you for good in everything.
   We answer your call.
Lord Christ, you left your glory and came to save our troubled world.
   We praise your Name.
You call us to carry your Cross with courage, and to share in your
      victory over sin and death.
   We answer your call.
Life-giving Spirit, you are patiently guiding our stubborn wills.
   We praise your Name.
You call us to share the grief of this world, to be channels of your
      gentleness.
   We answer your call.
Glory be to the Father, and to the Son, and to the Holy Spirit:
as it was in the beginning, is now, and shall be for ever. *Amen.*

Ascension Day

God our Father, King of heaven,
  all honour and glory and power are yours by right.

Jesus Christ, crucified, risen, ascended Lord,
  all honour and glory and power are yours by right.

Holy Spirit, witness that Jesus is glorified,
  all honour and glory and power are yours by right.

Our glorious and holy God, we praise you,
for all that makes the unseen heaven
a reality to us while we live on earth:
for Word and Sacrament,
for faithful Christians past and present,
for fellowship in the Church,
and for times of deep awareness
that Jesus is with us still.

All honour and glory and power are yours by right,
our Lord and our God. *Amen.*

Confession

Father, forgive us for our lack of vision, when we confine our
attention to this world and its needs, and forget the eternal,
unseen world. Forgive us when we glory in the reality of heaven,
but do little or nothing to bring a glimpse of that reality to sufferers
on earth. Forgive us our poor discipleship and our unwillingness to
live our lives here as citizens of heaven. Give us such a vision of
Jesus triumphant, that we may know he has destroyed our sins and
longs to make us like him. We ask it for his sake. *Amen.*

Ascension Day

Thanksgiving and Dedication

Heavenly Father, we join with saints and angels,
to thank you for the Lord Jesus Christ,
for his glory with you before the world was made,
for his earthly life, his bodily growth,
his mental and spiritual development.
We thank you that he shared our needs and anxieties,
our pains and our death.
He has conquered sin and death for us,
and has re-entered his native heaven to pray for us.

We thank you that he who lived among us
is now above us:
above us as One who is worthy at all times of worship and wonder;
above us as our Lord and our Director;
above us as our great Example.

We thank you too that, through the Holy Spirit,
he is constantly with us, at work in our lives.

We offer ourselves to you in his Name.
May we always strive to follow his example, to obey his
    commands,
and to worship him with you and the Holy Spirit
all the days of our life and throughout eternity;
for his Name's sake. *Amen.*

Sixth Sunday after Easter

Adoration

Mighty God, transcending your world yet dwelling within it,
   we worship you.
Caring Father, showing us in Jesus your face of love,
   we worship you.
We have no words with which to praise your great and glorious
   Name,
   only silence.
   Yet silence is not enough.
Lift us, hearts, minds and wills, into the joy of your divine
   presence,
that seeing you as you are, we may worship you as we ought;
through Jesus Christ our Lord. *Amen.*

Confession

Loving Father, we confess how much we have failed you and each
   other.
You have given us tasks to do –
   but we have not done them.
You have taught us to love one another –
   but our love has been cold.
You have bidden us hope –
   but we have despaired.
You have shown us the humility of Christ –
   but we have been proud.
You have given to those in need –
   but we have ignored them.
You have called us to trust –
   but we have not listened.

And yet we still have hope, and our hope is in Jesus.
By his incarnation and sharing of our lot,

forgive us our sins.
By his death on Calvary's Cross, which was for us,
    forgive us our sins.
By his rising again and his pleading for us in heaven,
    forgive us our sins.
Make us anew, in the image of the living Christ,
to your praise and glory. *Amen.*

Thanksgiving and Dedication

We thank you, God our Father, for the victory of our Lord Jesus
Christ over death and sin. We rejoice that we can come to you in
full assurance of faith and find you ever near. We are glad because
Jesus, priest and victim, is now our reigning King. We thank you
that all our prayers and praises can be brought in his Name and
that you hear us for his sake.

We thank you, God our Father, for all those whose lives reveal the
grace and love of Christ, those in whom we clearly see his
influence, and those who first taught us to follow his way. We
thank you for the power of Christ at work in human life, changing
fear into faith, despair into hope, injury into pardon.

Father, since through Jesus Christ your Son you have welcomed
and accepted us, grant us power to give ourselves anew to you.
May we so live in Christ now that we may look forward with hope
to sharing heaven's praise; through Christ our Lord. *Amen.*

Pentecost (Whitsunday)
(1st set)

Adoration

Let all the world praise you this day, Holy Spirit of God,
power of the Father come to claim our lives,
grace of the Son come to perfect us.
Through you comes the energy by which the world is made,
the stars are formed, the great galaxies are spread throughout
    space,
the light shines and darkness is overcome.

Through you comes the gift of life breathed into every human
    being,
so that we belong to the Father and can find our peace only with
    him.

Through you come the visions of the young and the dreams of the
    old,
the strong words of the prophets and the preachers,
the joyous songs of the psalmists,
the teaching and commands of the Lord.
Through you the scriptures bear their witness.
Through you comes the life of the Church, the vitality of the faith,
the healing of our bodies and minds and spirits.
You make your people holy.

Through you comes our confidence for the future,
our trust in your full purpose,
our assurance in God.

Glory be to you, Holy Spirit, Lord and giver of life,
from all who were and are and ever shall be, world without end.
    Amen.

Pentecost

Confession

[handwritten: O Lord as we gather here in your Name we raise ourselves to your service]

[handwritten left margin: you said]

There will be visions and dreams.
> But we are stuck in our ways, for we have stopped dreaming.
> Forgive us, Lord.
> *Holy Spirit, come, bless us.*

[handwritten: your best for us]

The believers were together.
> But we are so divided.
> Forgive us Lord.
> *Holy Spirit, come, bless us.*

There were sounds of wind and sight of fire.
> But we expect nothing to change, nothing new to happen.
> Forgive us, Lord.
> *Holy Spirit, come, bless us.*

They spoke with new freedom.
> But we are so tongue-tied, too dumb to speak for you.
> Forgive us, Lord.
> *Holy Spirit, come, bless us.*

Everyone heard the message.
> But we try to reach only the nearest few.
> Forgive us, Lord.
> *Holy Spirit, come, bless us.*

The Father will send another Helper.
> But we are so self-sufficient, relying on our own resources.
> Forgive us, Lord.
> *Holy Spirit, come, bless us.*

The Helper will teach you everything.
> But we have stopped wanting to learn or grow.
> Forgive us, Lord..
> *Holy Spirit, come, bless us. Amen.*

Thanksgiving and Dedication

We thank you, Holy Spirit of God,
sharing in all creation
from the very beginning of space and time and matter.
We thank you, by whom Mary was chosen;

114

Jesus was born and anointed and filled;
he embraced suffering and death and was glorified;
the Church was born.

We thank you, Holy Spirit of God,
for life transformed and made new –
for old thoughts giving way to new dreams;
old ways giving place to the new life in Christ;
old sins giving way to new graces;
old caution giving way to new courage;
old fears giving way to new confidence.

We thank you for your new life amongst the first disciples,
for Peter and James and John,
transformed by you.
We thank you for the new life amongst the next followers,
in Paul and Barnabas and Timothy.
We thank you for the long succession of followers and saints
stretching down the ages,
all made new by your power.
We thank you for those who trained us in the faith,
and called us to that new life.

Holy Spirit, ever making life new,
the living power of Christ within us,
come, claim us for yourself.
Yours we are,
now and every day,
for the rest of our lives,
into eternity.

Thanks be to God! *Amen.*

Pentecost (Whitsunday)
(2nd set)

Adoration

God the Father – Lord of all time and space,
   by whom we are created,
   to whom we belong,
   for whom we live –
   we adore you.

God the Son – alive with the life of God,
   revealing God to us in human form –
   we adore you.

God the Holy Spirit – breathing life into all creation,
   leading us into all truth –
   we adore you.

Holy Spirit of God,
   breathe upon us now and inspire our worship
   so that we may be filled with praise and thanksgiving.
Lord Jesus Christ,
   call us to your service,
   and lead us to know God as Father.
Father God,
   guard us and guide us;
   forgive us and help us;
   and bring us at last to your kingdom. *Amen.*

Confession

Father God, we confess that we have stifled your Spirit within us

You have sent us the Spirit of love,
   but we have preferred to hate those who oppose us.
You have sent us the Spirit of joy,
   but we have taken your gifts for granted and been ungrateful.

116

You have sent us the Spirit of peace,
  but we have allowed our selfishness to cause division and
    disharmony.
You have sent us the Spirit of patience,
  but we have been worried and anxious when we have not seen
    immediate results from our efforts, or evidence of your love.
You have sent us the Spirit of kindness,
  but we have been indifferent to other people's needs.
You have sent us the Spirit of goodness,
  but through our thoughtlessness, as well as our deliberate
    wrong-doing, we have sinned.
You have sent us the Spirit of faithfulness,
  but we have been fickle in our resolve, unreliable disciples of
    Jesus.
You have sent us the Spirit of gentleness,
  but we have been insensitive to the feelings of others.
You have sent us the Spirit of self-control,
  but we have lived recklessly, without disciplining ourselves.

Forgive us, Father God.
Teach us how much we need the power of your Spirit in our lives;
and breathe new life into us;
for Jesus Christ's sake. *Amen.*

Thanksgiving and Dedication

We thank you, Lord God, that you have always been at work in
your creation.
At the beginning of time your Spirit gave form and order to the
universe.
By your Spirit, the men and women of old were led to fulfil your
promises, and speak out in your Name.

Through your Spirit, Jesus was born of Mary,
and lived as a man among us.
It was your Spirit who led him to die for us on the Cross,
so that we might be free from the chains of sin and death.
You raised him from the dead,
and he ascended to your right hand in glory,
so that through him your Holy Spirit might be poured forth upon
  all people,

drawing them into the fellowship of your Church,
and sending them out in your Name
to proclaim the Gospel in word and deed
in every corner of the earth.

Through your Spirit, we have been brought out of darkness into
    your glorious light,
and enabled to call you Father.
Come again, Lord God, and breathe your Spirit into us.
Forgive us our sin,
comfort us when we are sad,
strengthen us when we are weak,
and guide us when we are strong.
Make us the people you want us to be;
through Jesus Christ our Lord. *Amen.*

Trinity Sunday (1st Sunday after Pentecost)
(Year 1)

Adoration

Our great and mighty God, Father, Son, and Holy Spirit:
when we consider your majesty and the works of your hand,
how insignificant we are;
And yet you have given us the capacity to know
that you are our creator and our Saviour,
that in you we live and move and have our being.
We cannot comprehend these mysteries,
but we know that as we worship and adore you
our lives are enriched
and our desire for communion with you is quickened.
Accept, great God, our prayer of adoration,
to the glory of your holy Name. *Amen.*

Confession

Father, we confess that we do not think enough of your mighty
acts of creation; of the life, death and resurrection of our Lord
Jesus Christ; of your gift of the Holy Spirit. We take so much for
granted until things go wrong; even then, we are often reluctant to
come to you, sometimes because of our lack of trust in you, or
because we believe we ought to be able to sort ourselves out. We
forget that you are more ready to give than we are to ask, and that
your offer of pardon is always available to those who are truly
sorry. Help us, through your grace, to know true repentance and
the joy of your forgiveness; for the sake of Jesus Christ our
Saviour. *Amen.*

Trinity Sunday

Thanksgiving and Dedication

Gracious God, we thank you for this world,
upon which you have bestowed so much variety of beauty and
    colour.
Words cannot express our wonder
when we think of the heavenly bodies moving in concert with our
    earthly planet;
the mighty seas, icebergs, mountains and deserts;
your handiwork in the tiniest insects and flowers.

Above all, we are thankful that you are our Father,
that your Son is our Saviour,
who was born among us,
and lived and died and rose again to redeem us,
and that through the Holy Spirit
we have the power to fulfil our part in your plan.
Our hearts burn with gratitude
that we have received your Gospel of salvation
and the assurance of your constant care for us.

So we dedicate ourselves
to responsible stewardship of all that you have given us,
and we pray that we may experience and reveal
the peace, the joy and the freedom
of lives lived according to your will;
for the sake of Jesus Christ our Lord. *Amen.*

Trinity Sunday (1st Sunday after Pentecost) *(Year 2)*

Adoration

God almighty, immortal, invisible,
whose Being is far beyond human thought and understanding,
we praise you for revealing yourself as Father, Son, and Holy
    Spirit –
Three Persons and yet One God.

God the Father, you created the universe in all its vastness and
    variety.
You made us in your own image,
and, when we fell into sin,
you sent your Son, the Lord Jesus Christ, to be our Saviour.
We worship and adore you.

God the Son, for our salvation you came to this earth,
lived a life of love,
died for us on the Cross,
rose from the dead,
and gave us the gift of the Holy Spirit.
We worship and adore you.

God the Holy Spirit, you come into our lives,
transforming, renewing, strengthening,
guiding us into the way of Christ.
You call us into the life of faith
and gather us, with all the people of God,
into the fellowship of Christ's Church.
We worship and adore you.

Triune God – One in Three and Three in One – we worship and
    adore you.
May all glory and praise be yours, now and for ever. *Amen.*

Trinity Sunday

Confession

Lord God, as we contemplate the glory, wonder and perfection of
   your being,
we are acutely aware of our own sin and unworthiness.

We confess that often our heavenly vision is obstructed by worldly
   desires,
our obedience to your will is overruled by self-indulgence,
our compassion is stifled by fear of involvement.

Forgive us that, in our folly, blindness and self-imprisonment,
we lead impoverished lives,
when the immeasurable riches of your grace in Christ Jesus
are freely available to all who put their trust in him.

In humble faith we would claim his promises and enter into his joy,
to his praise and glory. *Amen.*

Thanksgiving and Dedication

Eternal God, we thank you for the many ways in which you make
   yourself known.

We see your creative power in the wonderful world we live in.
We discover your loving purpose in the life, death, and
   resurrection of Jesus.
We experience your transforming presence in the indwelling
   Spirit.
We find you in the worship of your Church and in the simple faith
   of your saints.

We thank you for the writers, translators, and expositors of the
   Bible and for the truth the Spirit reveals to us in your word.
We thank you for those who have wrestled with theological
   problems and who, in their writing, teaching, and preaching,
   have given us fresh insights.
We thank you for the good news of the Gospel message, and we
   pray for strength and grace
   to proclaim it with our lips and in our lives,
   for the sake of Jesus Christ our Lord. *Amen.*

Second Sunday after Pentecost
(Year 1)

Adoration

Lord, we acknowledge that you are our God, one everlasting
    Lord,
Father, Son, and Holy Spirit.

God our Father, our Creator, we worship you.
Before time began
you spoke the word which brought light and life,
all colour, movement and variety.

God the Son, Lord Jesus Christ, we worship you.
You have come to us, living in our world,
proclaiming the truth,
and opening up the kingdom of God,
by your death and resurrection,
to all who believe in you.

God the Holy Spirit, we worship you.
You have come to us,
liberating our beings to praise you
and our minds to know your truth.
You have called us
and given us a place among the people of God.
You enable us to use our talents and abilities
in your praise and service.

Father, Son, and Holy Spirit, we worship and adore you. *Amen.*

Confession

We confess to you, Father, our unwillingness to respond to your
word, and our failure to enter wholeheartedly into our devotions.
You know how feeble has been our trust in you, how unloving we

have been; you know that those around us have been turned away from you by what we have done and said.

We confess that we have been slow to draw upon the resources of your Spirit, when, as your people, we have been faced with misunderstanding, prejudice, abuse, and scorn.

We praise you, Father, that you have not abandoned us because of what we are, but have illuminated our way with the light of your word and assured us of your continual presence. Forgive us our sin, and make us grateful for our high calling; through Jesus Christ our Lord. *Amen.*

Thanksgiving and Dedication

Lord God Almighty,
you have created all things and made us in your image.
We give you thanks because you have called us together in this
    fellowship,
and given us your Name to bear before all the world,
so that your loving nature might be revealed.

We thank you for the inspiration that comes to us
through the life and teaching of Jesus,
his sacrifice upon the Cross,
his triumph over evil, sin and death;
and for the encouragement that we receive
from the saints who have gone before us.
We thank you for your promise
that you will fill us with your Spirit,
to inspire us with a vision of your kingdom,
to re-assure us of your continual presence,
and to make us worthy of our calling.

Lord God, we are your people,
committed to your service;
in the Name of Jesus Christ our Lord. *Amen.*

Second Sunday after Pentecost
(Year 2)

Adoration

Living God, Lord of creation, sustainer of what you have made,
we worship you for your strength.
With you there is no variation, no change;
you are utterly reliable.

We rejoice in you, the rock of our salvation,
the sure ground of our faith.
We praise you that it is upon your strength and purpose
that your Church is founded,
the Church which is the Body of Christ,
the embodiment of your word to us.
We praise you for the unity of the Godhead,
for the fellowship of Three in One.

Grant that we may worship today in the unity of Christ;
we ask it for his sake. *Amen.*

Confession

Loving, caring Father,
we confess before you our division and dissension
and the frailties we have created within Christ's Body, the Church.

We confess that we have been jealous for our rights and lax in
    fulfilling our duties;
that we have been narrow in our view of the kingdom, not seeing
    our Lord;
that we have not loved one another as Christ has loved us;
that we have been unwilling to give of ourselves in fellowship.

We ask you to forgive our poor service of your Church.
Match our poverty with your riches, we pray,
and make us powerful to live as you have called us to live;
for the benefit of others and to your praise and glory.
We ask it in the Name of Jesus Christ our Lord. *Amen.*

Thanksgiving and Dedication

Almighty God, we thank you for creating and sustaining the
world; and for revealing your love to us in Jesus Christ, your Son.
We thank you for his life and death and resurrection and
ascension, through which you promise the forgiveness of sins and
the gift of the Holy Spirit to us, and to our children, and to all who
are far away, everyone whom you, our God, may call.

We thank you for your Church, through which you have spoken to
us, into which you have called us, in which you have brought
purpose to our lives and hope of life eternal.

We thank you that in the Church there are those who put the
world to shame, who give and do not look for reward, who reveal
you to others and bring reconciliation and peace.

We thank you that within your Church there are signs of growth
towards unity, that there is evidence of warmth and fellowship,
and an increasing recognition of the Church's common purpose.

Almighty God, we cherish our place in your Church. We pray that
its divisions may be healed. And we offer ourselves to serve within
its fellowship, that we may foster that unity in Christ which is your
will for us all; for our Saviour's sake. *Amen.*

Third Sunday after Pentecost
(Year 1)

Adoration

Lord God, we praise you'
   because in you is life and joy and love.
We worship you
   because your life is always new and you sustain us by your
     vitality.
We love you
   because you always care, but never stifle.

Heavenly Father, we serve you
   because you share our troubles and lighten our burdens.
We follow you
   because you offer us a way of living,
   but always break out of our attempts to confine you in our
     descriptions and by our intellect.
We adore you
   because you accept us in our sinfulness,
   in order to break the power of sin within us.

Praise God, who loves us,
through Jesus Christ, who saves us,
and who raises us to a new life of fellowship in his Spirit! *Amen.*

Confession

Lord Jesus,
you are the true Vine and we are the branches.
But we confess that we become separated from you
   by wilfulness – when we seek our own satisfaction;
   by forgetfulness – when we neglect the means of grace;
   by aimlessness – when we are carried along by life's routines;

Third Sunday after Pentecost

   by self-centredness – when we look inward at our own needs and
     problems, but do not look outward on what is true, wonderful
     and loving.

Assure us, Lord Jesus,
of your forgiveness for our past faults.
Keep us connected to your living presence;
and, by your power flowing continually through us,
sustain us in the life to which we have been baptized.
For your Name's sake we ask it. *Amen.*

Thanksgiving and Dedication

Heavenly Father, creator of the world,
who made us in your own image,
we thank you for revealing your will for us:

   for the law and the commandments
   and the positive social relationships made possible when they
     are observed;
   for the prophets in every age
   who have sought to defend the exploited and to promote justice;
   for Jesus, who ministered to the poor,
   and, by his death and resurrection,
   gave his followers power to live triumphantly.
We thank you for his assurance of rescue from all that binds us,
and for evidence of changed lives,
of harmful habits broken,
and of new challenges undertaken.

And now we re-dedicate ourselves to your service, Father,
as we recall the vows
made on our behalf at baptism,
willingly endorsed by us at our confirmation,
and sustained by this congregation;
and we pray
   that we may die to sin and be raised to the new life in Christ;
   that we may maintain the common life of worship and service as
     members of the household of faith;
   and that the good work you have begun in us
   may be confirmed by the continued working of your Holy Spirit;
   through Jesus Christ our Lord. *Amen.*

Third Sunday after Pentecost
(Year 2)

Adoration

Eternal God and Father,
in you is the source of all life,
the fount of all wisdom,
the well-spring of all grace.
Your days are without end;
your loving mercies without number.

We depend on you;
and we remember your goodness to us
and to those who have gone before us.
We tell your story in every generation:
you are our familiar God,
God of Abraham, Isaac and Jacob,
God and Father of our Lord Jesus Christ,
God of a pilgrim people, your Church.

But you are not our captive God,
not a god of our own making,
not bound by us, not controlled by us.

Ahead of us, leading us,
guiding us and calling us,
you are the Lord God,
the all-wise, all-compassionate.

To you we lift up our hearts
and we worship you,
one God for ever and ever. *Amen.*

Third Sunday after Pentecost

Confession

Father,
we rejoice in your dependability
throughout all ages.
Nothing can separate us from your love
in Jesus Christ our Lord.
Relying on that love we turn to you
in penitence and faith;
moved by your holiness,
we confess our sin.

You call us to place our confidence in you.
You have assured us of eternal life in Christ.
You have declared us to belong to you
in the sign of baptism,
and you have poured your Spirit into our lives.

But only with great timidity do we call you 'Father'.
We hesitate to claim Christ as Lord.
We keep the Spirit's gifts to ourselves.

Assure us again, good Lord, of your goodness.
Make us afresh to be your living Church.
Raise in us a hymn of praise
that we may be joyful children of a loving Father;
through Jesus Christ our Lord. *Amen.*

Thanksgiving and Dedication

Lord God,
whenever we hear your story
we remember and recognize your presence:
the same God, yesterday, today and forever.

You placed men and women
at the heart of your creation,
and all you provided for us is good.
You dared to give us
co-responsibility with you for life itself.

Time and time again –
through prophet and patriarch,
through faithful men and women –
you recalled your people
to your loving purposes for them.
At the right time
your Son Jesus Christ lived our life,
died our death, and raised us up;
and through his Spirit
we call you Father.

Out of our fragmented world
you called a people to be your Church,
slave and free, native and alien,
male and female,
all one in Christ Jesus,
signs of your drawing all to yourself
in your coming kingdom.

Today we thank you
for the power of Jesus to heal and save;
we rejoice with those who come to him,
openly or in secret;
and we praise you for the faith
which makes us whole.

Father,
fill us with your Spirit,
that we may boldly declare
your love for us
in Jesus Christ our Lord. *Amen.*

Fourth Sunday after Pentecost
(Year 1)

Adoration

Blessed be the Lord the God of Israel
and blessed be his glorious Name for ever;
blessed in his love before time began
and blessed in the holiness of his kingdom;
blessed in the redemption of the Cross
and blessed in the descent of the Spirit;
blessed in the songs of the saints
and blessed in the praises of his children.
Blessed be the Lord the God of Israel
from everlasting to everlasting. *Amen.*

Confession

Lord God, most merciful and most holy,
we confess to you
our lack of response to your caring love
and our feeble grasp of your great promise.
Look upon our proud hearts with the eyes of your compassion
and embrace us with the arms of your mercy.
Pardon our faults for we admit them
and forgive our sins for we repent of them.
Restore to us again the joy of your salvation
and renew our lives with the power of your Holy Spirit;
through Jesus Christ our Lord. *Amen.*

Thanksgiving and Dedication

Almighty God,
in whom alone we find our chief delight
and our deepest joy;
accept this act of thanksgiving
for the many signs of your great love in the world about us;
accept this act of praise
for the redemption of your people through Jesus Christ our Lord;
accept this act of worship
for the sending of your Spirit upon the Church universal;
accept this act of response
for the freedom we have found in the proclamation of your holy
　Gospel;
and to you, Father,
we give ourselves again;
open our lips to declare the wonders of your love,
enter into our lives that they may witness to your truth,
and fill our hearts that they may be the dwelling-place of your
　eternal Spirit;
to whom with you, Father, and your only-begotten Son,
we render all honour and glory
now and for ever. *Amen.*

Fourth Sunday after Pentecost
(Year 2)

Adoration

Lord God, our heavenly Father,
we praise and adore you;
we celebrate your mighty power and your love.

You have guided and preserved us in all our ways;
you are worthy of all praise and honour and love.

Your glory is beyond all thought:
you are alpha and omega, the first and the last;
you are beyond all letters and all words,
beyond all that we can say or think.

Accept our praise and adoration, we pray,
through the merits of your Son,
our Saviour Jesus Christ. *Amen.*

Confession

God our Father, we confess before you all our failures and
shortcomings, and especially as members of your Church. We
have been lukewarm in your service: by failures of example and
neglect of opportunity we have undermined the great mission of
spreading the gospel of love. We have been preoccupied with our
other gods of materialism and self-interest; forgive us, Lord, our
disloyalty and distraction. Transform the feebleness of our will and
the poverty of our effort, and send us out to preach your word in
all we say and do; through your Son, Jesus Christ our Lord. *Amen.*

Thanksgiving and Dedication

Almighty God, we give you thanks for all your goodness to us.
You have created and preserved us,
and sent your Son to redeem us;
he lived our life; he died our death;
he rose again to bring us to eternal life.
Through him you have poured out your Holy Spirit on your
    people.
Especially at this time we give thanks for your Church and those
    who serve in it,
and your word and those who preach it.
May we know the truth of the gospel of salvation,
and may we always hold fast to it;
may we, through our different gifts,
bring the message of your love to every person who needs it.
We dedicate ourselves, Lord, to them,
remembering especially those who do not know that message of
    love
and those who have forgotten it:
may we always be ready to receive those who need us,
and those who are returning to the faith;
may we rejoice with them in their new life,
and so set an example that others may be turned to your truth;
for the sake of Jesus Christ our Lord. *Amen.*

Fifth Sunday after Pentecost
(Year 1)

Adoration

True God, Father of our Lord Jesus Christ, you will not share our love and loyalty with another. In worship we concentrate our minds on you now, we offer our deep-felt longings, and we give ourselves to you, that our worship may be an act of love. Make us and keep us single-minded in your service.

We seek to adore you through our interests and commitments in society. By respecting others and giving service to them in the way we would wish to receive it, may we honour you.

We seek to adore you through friendship and marriage. By loving those close to us with sensitivity and appreciation, may we come to know and celebrate your love more truly.

We seek to adore you through our membership and ministry in your Church. Help us to see the Church as divine as well as human, broadcasting your love to the world and transmitting our love to you.

As we worship you now, we abandon and deny any lesser gods who have gained our allegiance. We will not bow down to them or worship them, for they are mere images. They keep us in slavery while you give us freedom by your law of love. Help us to desire you alone and to worship you with undivided hearts; through Jesus Christ our Lord. *Amen.*

Confession

We confess to you, eternal God, that we have not loved as Christ loved us. Our self-offering has been grudging and incomplete. Indecency in thought and action and greed for gain have spoiled our society and our part in it. We have been persuaded by shallow arguments; we have lost our hold on Christ and his kingdom.

We ask to be forgiven, and brought out of the shadows into the broad light of day. As we live in the light, may goodness spring up in the place of barrenness. May our growing sense of justice help us to see what is truly pleasing to you, and may the encouragement of your Spirit help us to do it; for Christ's sake. *Amen.*

Thanksgiving and Dedication

Father, receive our thanksgiving for your glorious gift of life and all that makes living worthwhile. We celebrate the life that is more than basic breathing – the life of keen awareness, faith's perception, and mutually committed love.

We thank you for Jesus, who showed us the full potential of human life, lived in perfect obedience to your will. For his coming and for his living, for his dying and for his rising, for his exaltation and for your sending of the Holy Spirit in his Name, we give you thanks and praise.

We thank you for constantly recalling us to a right mind:
  when we fail to keep your commandments
  you patiently restore us to a right relationship with you;
  when we hold back and hesitate in your service
  you challenge us to go the whole way in commitment;
  when we cling to our wealth and our other false securities
  you invite us to risk all for Christ's sake.

Help us to progress beyond reasonableness and reserve.
Make us more daring in the attempt to step beyond our
    divided loyalties
into the place of your presence.
Help us to smile at impossibilities
and prove them possible as we enter your kingdom;
through Jesus Christ our Lord. *Amen.*

Fifth Sunday after Pentecost
(Year 2)

Adoration

Lord God, we worship and adore you.

Your holiness is beyond our understanding;
your majesty is beyond our imagination;
your love is greater than we can conceive.
But you have revealed yourself to us
through our experience of creation and the opportunities of life,
and in the life and death and resurrection of Jesus,
so that we can affirm
that it is by you that we have come to be;
it is to you that everyone owes allegiance;
your kingdom enfolds all people of every age, every race, every
    colour, and every tongue,
and it is in your will that all find their peace.

Father of us all, you care for each of your children
and you know us all by name:
as your family we celebrate together,
knowing that we are secure in your love.

We worship you; we honour you;
we adore you; we thank you;
through Jesus Christ our Lord. *Amen.*

Confession

Lord God, we confess to you the sins of the world
of which we are a part:
    we confess that we have misused the resources you have given
        us,
    and spoilt your world through our greed;
    we have treated one another unfairly,

and exploited the weakest among us;
we have regarded wealth more highly than people,
and valued others for what they have, or can produce,
rather than for what they are;
we have allowed hatred, fear and suspicion to divide us.
Forgive us, we pray, for Jesus' sake.

And we confess to you our individual sins:
Through ignorance, thoughtlessness and prejudice
we have caused others harm, and we regret it.
Sometimes we have consciously wronged others,
in what we have done or said or thought,
or in what we have failed to do.
Forgive us, we pray, for Jesus' sake.

(Silence)

Father, help us to know the peace of your forgiving love.
Give us, we pray, courage to try to make amends where we have
    failed
and the power to live as brothers and sisters of one another,
as your children in the world;
for Jesus Christ's sake. *Amen.*

Thanksgiving and Dedication

Almighty God,
we thank you that all human beings are born into your family,
and that you have shown us that it is your will
that we should live together in peace,
with mutual co-operation, understanding, and respect.

We thank you that, when, in our blindness and stupidity,
we ignored your laws,
and through our selfishness caused one another to be lonely, sad,
    and afraid,
you sent Jesus to show us your will for us,
and to release us from our sin.
In his ministry of love and care,
in his death and in his resurrection,
he broke the power of evil and exposed the folly of our divisions,
and he is exalted to your right hand in glory.

We thank you that he called all people into the fellowship of his
 Church,
and gave them a vision of your kingdom,
in which there should be no distinctions
of race, or sex, or wealth, or class.

We thank you that, by the power of the Spirit,
the Church now reaches all round the world
as a symbol of your family;
as a testimony to the reconciling power of your love;
as a witness to the Gospel of Jesus, your Son.

May we and all your Church work and pray for the day
when all people will know themselves to be your children,
and recognize one another as members of your family;
through Jesus Christ our Lord. *Amen*.

Sixth Sunday after Pentecost

Adoration

Mighty God, we meet to celebrate your greatness.
We join with the hosts of heaven
to sing your praises and to offer you worship.
For you are worthy of adoration from every mouth,
and every tongue should praise you.
You created the earth by your power;
you save the human race by your mercy,
and make it new by your grace.
Father, Son, and Holy Spirit,
we offer you our grateful praise. *Amen.*

Confession

Holy God, we are ashamed before you.
We recognize that we have no right to be here,
except that through Jesus Christ you bid us come,
and assure us of your love.

Forgive us that we take such grace and mercy so lightly:
we are selfish and arrogant,
we reject our Christian discipleship and neglect each other's
    needs.
We are content to live passively amid injustice and apostasy,
such is our moral inertia.
Our apathy extends to the prayers we say:
we are half-hearted and unmoved, even in your presence.
We take your free grace as if it were cheap.

We need forgiveness.
We need to be made new.
Help us to grasp the amazing truth that even now,
despite lethargy and failure,
your grace is for us;

that forgiveness is possible,
such is your love;
through Jesus Christ our Lord. *Amen.*

Thanksgiving and Dedication

We thank you, Father, for your gracious love to your faithless
    children;
for the creation and preservation of the heavens and the earth;
and your constant faithfulness to humankind.
We thank you for Jesus Christ:
    for the example of his life,
    the truth of his words,
    the wonder of his death,
    and the power of his resurrection;
    for the privilege of following him
    and living the new life he offers.
We thank you for the Holy Spirit,
the inspirer of faith and revealer of truth.
We thank you for the Church, and for our place within it;
for members of the Church who have shown to us,
by their living and their dying,
your renewing and transforming power in human lives.

Accept our thanks, Father;
accept our love for you,
and our lives dedicated to you.
Lead us onward, and continue your renewing work in us;
for the sake of Jesus Christ our Lord. *Amen.*

Seventh Sunday after Pentecost

Adoration

Eternal God, into the peace of your presence
we bring our restless lives.
Down through the ages men and women have sought you
and found that your faithfulness has no end.
Your people long ago journeyed by your guidance
and rested on your love.
So guide us as a pillar of cloud by day and fire by night,
that our imaginations may be filled with your beauty,
our minds fired by your truth,
and our hearts overflowing with your love;
for without you life has no source, or purpose, or destiny.
Refresh our faith, restore our confidence,
and lay your guiding hand on our lives.
We ask this through Jesus Christ our Lord. *Amen.*

Confession

Loving heavenly Father,
you are so far above us that we cannot fully understand you,
and yet so deep within us that you know our closest secrets.
We come to seek your forgiveness.

Forgive us those occasions when love has not been the guiding
principle of our lives.
Forgive us when we have been impatient with others, unkind and
envious.
Forgive us when we have been boastful or rude or selfish or quick
to take offence.
Forgive us those occasions when our love has grown cold and lost
its faith and its hope and its endurance.

Seventh Sunday after Pentecost

God our Father, forgive our sins,
lead us away from our pride and conceit,
enlarge our thought,
and make us more compassionate and sympathetic to others.
We ask this through Jesus Christ our Lord. *Amen.*

Thanksgiving and Dedication

Lord God, we come to you today with praise and thankfulness,
and commit our lives once more into your keeping.
We thank you for friends who have loved us,
for fellow Christians from whom we have learned so much,
and for the height and depth of our human experience.
We bring our gratitude to you for the glimpses of the eternal
that come to us through the beauty of nature,
the words of scripture, and the love and kindness of others.

Above all, we thank you for Jesus,
for his birth and ministry, his death and resurrection,
his exaltation to glory, and the power of his Spirit;
and for those great moments of revelation,
deep within our own lives,
when we have felt our hearts moved,
our spirits lifted,
our confidence restored,
and our sins forgiven.

And so, as we step forward into the unknown,
make us brave and courageous
and give us a sense of fellowship with the saints of every age.
So we may encourage all who journey with us in this life.
We ask this in the Name of Jesus Christ our Lord. *Amen.*

Eighth Sunday after Pentecost

Adoration

Almighty God, you have made us in your image
and you are the very breath of our life.

We praise you that you have raised us from our sin
to a new quality of life and of living.

We praise you for your Spirit,
who calls us, and then equips us for your service.
We praise you for the work of your Spirit in the Church and in the
    world,
constantly redeeming and renewing your creation.

We praise you that your Spirit is in our midst as we worship you
    today.
Breathe upon the dry bones of our fellowship,
and make us your living, worshipping Body;
through Jesus Christ our Lord. *Amen.*

Confession

Spirit of truth,
    we confess that we have been shown your truth,
    but have not lived by it.
Spirit of wisdom,
    we confess our foolishness
    and our inflated estimate of our own abilities.
Spirit of discernment,
    we confess that we have been quick to judge
    and eager to cast the first stone.
Spirit of prophecy,
    we confess that we often ignore the cutting edge of your call.
    We prefer what is comfortable and familiar
        to the disturbing challenge which you offer us.

Eighth Sunday after Pentecost

Spirit of patience,
  we confess our lack of patience,
  our irritability, and our inability to control our tempers.
Spirit of peace,
  we confess our part in the hatred
  which divides nation from nation, and person from person.
Spirit of healing,
  we confess our need of the wholeness which only you can give.
Spirit of life,
  enable us to grasp fully and freely
  the eternal life you give to those who ask;
through Jesus Christ our Lord. *Amen.*

Thanksgiving and Dedication

Almighty God, we thank you for your creative Spirit,
who brooded over the face of the waters,
bringing order out of chaos.
We thank you for your life-giving Spirit,
who grants us our daily breath.

We thank you for your Spirit of power,
who called the prophets to proclaim your word of justice,
and to call your people to repentance.
We thank you for your Spirit of grace,
whose work was made manifest
in the life and death and resurrection of Jesus your Son.

We thank you for your Spirit of faith and hope and love.
May that Spirit who is the source of life,
direct our lives,
so that we may show forth his harvest day by day.
We ask it in the Name of Jesus Christ our Lord. *Amen.*

Ninth Sunday after Pentecost

Adoration

We praise you, great and gracious God,
Father, Son, and Holy Spirit.

We praise you, God the Father,
glorious and eternal ruler of time and space.
You made the universe and all that is in it;
you created men and women in your own image;
you graciously revealed your purpose and your love,
above all in your Son Jesus Christ.
We praise you, God the Father.

We praise you, God the Son.
You came to earth to reveal the Father's love.
We praise you for your humble birth;
for your ministry of teaching, preaching and healing;
for your death upon the Cross;
for your glorious resurrection and ascension;
for your continual intercession for us;
and for the gift of the Holy Spirit.
We praise you, God the Son.

We praise you, God the Holy Spirit,
source of all goodness, beauty and truth.
You are for ever with the people of Jesus,
guiding them, guarding them, leading them into all truth;
and you are with us now as we worship.
We praise you, God the Holy Spirit.

So we praise you, great and gracious God,
Father, Son, and Holy Spirit,
now and for ever. *Amen.*

Ninth Sunday after Pentecost

Confession

Father, forgive us,
What poor disciples of Jesus we are!
How badly our lives reflect his love!
How slow we are to follow in his steps!

Jesus forgave his enemies;
　　but we are vindictive and seek revenge.
Jesus never used force to achieve his objectives;
　　but we want our own way, whatever the means of attaining it
　　　　may be.
Jesus was silent before his accusers;
　　but we bluster and argue and squabble and fight.
Jesus prayed often and fervently for strength to resist evil;
　　but we have not prayed as we ought
　　and have expected painless results from our feeble efforts.

Father, forgive us.
Give us a true desire to fight against evil.
Show us that the only effective weapons for the struggle
are those which Jesus used.
So may we witness for him by the innocence of our behaviour;
our grasp of truth; our patience and kindliness;
by gifts of the Holy Spirit; by sincere love;
by declaring the truth; by the power of God.
We ask it for Christ's sake. *Amen*.

Thanksgiving and Dedication

Almighty Father, we give you thanks
that you have revealed your power and your glory
through your mighty acts of creation,
and that you have revealed your redeeming and transforming love
through your beloved Son.

We thank you for Jesus,
who lived and worked and suffered and died
for the sake of all the world,
and whom you raised again from death
to be praised and exalted above all for ever.

148

We thank you that you have called us to his service,
and that those whom you call
you also equip for their task.
We thank you for men and women in many times and places
who have struggled courageously against evil,
strengthened by your grace,
sustained by faith and hope and love.
We thank you for the realization that,
though by ourselves we can do nothing,
we can do all things in Christ who strengthens us.

Almighty Father, we re-dedicate our lives to you.
Give us, we pray, humility to acknowledge our need of your help;
faith to trust in your powerful love;
and courage to fight against evil within us and around us;
for the sake of Jesus Christ our Lord. *Amen*.

Tenth Sunday after Pentecost

Adoration

God of all power and might, ruler of the universe,
you are worthy of all praise.
You created the galaxies, the planets, and this earth.
You made us for yourself
and our hearts are restless till they find their rest in you.
You have given us wills with which to obey you
and voices to sing your praise.
May we find the purpose of our lives in doing your will
and in giving voice to the praise which all creation shows.
We ask it through Jesus Christ our Lord. *Amen.*

Confession

Almighty God, the praise we try to offer is spoilt
by our failure to do your will.
With our lips we have professed to follow Christ,
but you are not deceived.
You know that we have not shown his humble, self-emptying love;
we have not borne the burdens of others;
we have not had the mind of Christ.
Now we acknowledge our many sins;
we repent in dust and ashes.

Speak to us now, Father,
as your Son once spoke to a sinful woman,
and say to each of us
'Your sins are forgiven; go in peace.'
Help us, to whom so much has been forgiven, to love you more;
through Jesus Christ our Lord. *Amen.*

150

Thanksgiving and Dedication

Lord God, you spoke in the beginning and the world was made,
and you spoke in many and various ways through the prophets.

Now you have shown us your mind and purpose more fully in your
    Son:

he humbled himself
and became obedient unto death, death on a Cross;
therefore you have highly exalted him
and bestowed on him the Name which is above every name,
that in the Name of Jesus every knee should bow,
and every tongue confess that Jesus Christ is Lord.

Through him you have sent upon us the Holy Spirit,
the Lord, the giver of life,
and have made us citizens of heaven,
from which we await the Lord Jesus Christ,
when he who is our Saviour shall come to be our Judge.

We thank you for counting us worthy
to stand in your presence and to serve you,
and we pray you to accept our spiritual sacrifice
of praise and thanksgiving.

Send the Holy Spirit on your people,
that, being crucified with Christ,
we may be raised to life with him,
so that, with all your saints,
we may praise and glorify you for ever;
through Jesus Christ our Lord. *Amen.*

Eleventh Sunday after Pentecost

Adoration

Lord our God,
whose power is proclaimed   *in the beauty & wonder*
in the glory of the skies above us   *of creation*
and in the wonders of the world about us;
draw near to us in this act of praise
and open our eyes to see you in your beauty,
and our ears to hear the words of your heavenly wisdom;
open our minds to comprehend the truth that sets us free
and our hearts to embrace the love which passes all understanding;
through Jesus Christ our Lord. *Amen.*

Confession   150 2

Lord God, (most) merciful and (most) holy;
we confess to you
the greatness of our sin
and the commandments which we have broken;
we recall the still small voice which we have disobeyed
and the Christ within our neighbour
from whom we have turned aside.

In your great goodness
and for the sake of your only Son, our Saviour,
forgive us that which is past;
give us grace to be truly penitent
and to accept the good news of the Gospel
that we may enter into the joys of your eternal kingdom;
through Jesus Christ our Lord. *Amen.*

Thanksgiving and Dedication

We bless you, Lord our God,
that in your wisdom and love
you have created the heavens and the earth
and that you have given life and breath
to those whom you have fashioned for fellowship with yourself.

We give you thanks that at no time
have you left yourself without a witness to your grace
and that in every generation
you have raised up your saints and your servants
to proclaim the day of your salvation.

We bless you that in these last days
you have sent your Son, our Saviour Jesus Christ,
to be the servant of all
and to give his life as a ransom for many.
We bless you that by his death he has destroyed death
and that in his resurrection
he has brought life and immortality to light.

We give you thanks for the out-pouring of your Holy Spirit
whereby we are able to call you Father
and to serve you in the needs of one another.

Open our hearts, Lord,
and kindle within them
the flame of your own compassion,
that we may give ourselves afresh
to the needs of the community in which you have set us
and to the service of the world which Christ has redeemed.

Grant that, with all who look to you in hope,
we may see you at last in the glory of your heavenly light and
    splendour,
where you reign with your Son and the Holy Spirit,
one God, now and for ever. *Amen.*

Twelfth Sunday after Pentecost

Adoration

The God who made the world
is not far from any one of us.

Eternal God, in whom we live and move and have our being,
whose presence we know in this hour and in this place;
spanning the universe of time and space,
yet coming gladly to the humble heart;
desire of all nations, light of those who seek, home of the lost;
closer to us than mind or breath or memory or soul;
all-filling, all-ruling, all-loving;
unspeakably great – and shown to us in Jesus;
high and holy – and living in us in your Spirit;
in trembling awe we look up, and call you Father.

All glory is yours, Father.
And you,
you are ours. *Amen.*

Confession

Father and maker of us all,
you have called us to deal justly,
to love mercy,
and to walk humbly before you;
yet in our thoughtless lives,
in our divided and inward-looking churches,
in our inhuman, power-hungry society, of east and of west,
we turn away from you,
we betray your kindness,
we hide your truth in fearful hearts.

For all that, you gave us your Son,
who walked humbly with you,

gave his life in mercy,
and brought us the new righteousness of pardon,
to keep alight in the world the lamp of your compassion.

Forgive us, for his sake.
Rekindle in each one of us the light of faith,
revive your Church with the light of hope,
and hold up in our midst the light that will shine on everyone.
Lord, in your mercy,
Hear our prayer.

God was in Christ, reconciling the world to himself,
and entrusting to us the message of reconciliation.

Hear then his word of grace to us: Your sins are forgiven.
Amen. Thanks be to God.

Thanksgiving and Dedication

We lift up our hearts to you, our God and our Father,
we lift up our hearts in the Spirit, and we thank you,
for, having given us life and will and sense and reason,
you have offered your Son, that in him we might be a new
     creation.
For our sake you made him to be sin who knew no sin,
so that in him we might share your gracious victory over sin.

You have made us your witnessing people, your ambassadors in
     the world,
to speak for you to each other and to our neighbours,
to be your light in the darkness.

In faith, we give ourselves anew to you now in Jesus' Name,
that you may make us one as he is one with you in the Spirit,
one in the confession of your reconciling Gospel,
one in the care for our neighbours
that speaks your word in action,
one in the growing communion of joy
that reflects the love you share with your Son, with your Spirit.

That the world may believe, and discover your peace,
Lord our God, make us your own;
for Christ's sake. *Amen.*

Thirteenth Sunday after Pentecost

Adoration

God our Father, we praise you because you have shown us in Jesus
that you are not a distant and unfeeling God. We praise you that
he shared human life to the full, enduring bodily pain, mental
struggles, and temptation. He has revealed to us your love and
compassion for all who suffer. You are ours, a refuge and strength,
a very present help in trouble. Grant that in sorrow and pain, as
well as in joy and gladness, we may put our trust in you, and praise
you as we ought; through Jesus Christ our Lord. *Amen.*

Confession

Lord Jesus Christ, you pronounced a blessing on those who mourn
and those who are persecuted for righteousness' sake. Forgive us
that we so often turn away from situations that may cause us to
suffer. Pardon us for our compromise with evil – for the things we
have said and done, or failed to say and do, in the hope that we
might find ease and comfort. Forgive us our lack of concern for
those who suffer in the world today, and for all that we do,
knowingly or in ignorance, that brings suffering and pain to others.
Give us loving compassion for sufferers which is like your own; for
your holy Name's sake. *Amen.*

Thanksgiving and Dedication

Glory be to you, heavenly Father,
for your unchanging love which is revealed in all your works.

We thank you for patriarchs, prophets, and psalmists,
who, in times of sorrow and pain,
experienced the strength and fortitude that come from you.

We thank you for Jesus,
who endured the Cross for our salvation,
who was raised again triumphant,
whose wounds are yet visible above.

We thank you for apostles, evangelists, and martyrs,
who endured suffering and death for the sake of Christ,
who now reign with Jesus in glory.

We thank you for Christians who suffer heroically today,
the hungry, the persecuted, the disabled, and the permanently ill;
and for the inspiration that comes to us
as we read or hear of their courage.

Give us grace to take our share of suffering
as good soldiers of Jesus Christ,
and to share in his ministry to sufferers around us.
May we always remember
that in giving we receive, in forgiving we are forgiven,
in healing we are healed, and in dying we are born to eternal life.
We pray in the Name of Jesus Christ,
our crucified and risen Lord. *Amen.*

Fourteenth Sunday after Pentecost

Adoration

Ever-living God, source of power and love,
  all praise and glory belongs to you;
Ever-living God, source of forgiveness and hope,
  all praise and glory belongs to you;
Ever-living God, shown to us in Jesus your Son,
  all praise and glory belongs to you;
Ever-living God, constantly present in our lives by the Spirit,
  all praise and glory belongs to you;
Ever-living God, ceaselessly working in human history,
  all praise and glory belongs to you;
Ever-living God, head of your Church, guide of your people,
  all praise and glory belongs to you.

Lifting our voices before you, we sing your praise.
Lifting our hearts before you, we rejoice that you are God.
Lifting our lives before you, we pay you homage.
Accept the worship of your people, Lord,
to the praise and glory of your holy Name;
through Jesus Christ our Lord. *Amen.*

Confession

Merciful Father, in your presence,
and in the communion of your faithful people, living and departed,
we admit our faults.

You have taught us to love you with our whole being.

We confess that
  our discipleship has been lazy;
  we have been afraid of what others might think;
  we have missed opportunities for bearing witness;
  we have not loved you with our whole being.

You have taught us to love our neighbours as we love ourselves.

We confess that
    we have been envious of those who have more than we have;
    we have despised those who are different from us;
    we have been angry with those who disagree with us;
    we have not loved our neighbours as we love ourselves.

Merciful Father, we know that in Christ you love and forgive us.
You have made us your children and you will go on loving us.
Help us to live by the strength and hope this faith gives us.
Help us to overcome our sins and to trust you for the grace we
    need;
through Jesus Christ our Lord. *Amen.*

Thanksgiving and Dedication

Father God, the rich variety of your world makes us glad.
We thank you for the contrasts of nature:
    the ruggedness of mountains, the lushness of fields,
    the warmth of the sun and the coldness of snow,
    the challenge of the day and the peace of the night.

We thank you, too, for the contrasts among people,
    for individual personalities and gifts,
    for the fact that we are not all alike.
We thank you for people of other cultures and races
    and for all that we have to learn from them.
We thank you for giving us other people to care for,
    and a sense of responsibility for those in need.

Father God, we thank you for creating one world
    and for sending Jesus to live and work,
    to suffer and die, and to rise victorious from death,
    in order that he might break down the barriers between us
    and make us one in him.

Unite us in love and service, we pray,
    so that the whole earth may praise your Name;
    through Jesus Christ our Lord. *Amen.*

Fifteenth Sunday after Pentecost

Adoration

Dear God, supreme in all your loving,
you are like both a father and a mother to us.
    You surround us with your loving care,
    like a mother nestling her baby in her arms.
    Like a good parent, you supply our needs.
    You train us in the way of life.
    You give us our freedom.
    You listen to our troubles and our crying and our longing for
      comfort.
    You share with us the pain of our mistakes and our sins.

You are always welcoming us when we have rebelled or gone
      astray.
    You go to the uttermost lengths to win us back.
    You keep the house ever open
    and wait for us with outstretched arms.
    You share all your riches with us.
    You are always helping us to start all over again,
    made new by the power and cost of your loving.
    You are utterly reliable.

With you alone do we find our true home.
With all your people we belong to your great world-wide family.

Praise be to you, our God, father and mother to us all. *Amen.*

Confession

Forgive us, Lord,
that in the world, and in the Church, and in our homes, we live as
    sinners.
    We quarrel. We assert ourselves against each other.
    We will not give way or climb down.

We pit ourselves against the common good.
We are proud.

Forgive us, Lord, sinners that we are.
We pledge ourselves to each other and then falter in our
commitments.
We should be reliable, but we are often fickle.
We should encourage each other, but we often tell tales, spread
gossip, play fast and loose with our affections.

Forgive us, Lord, sinners that we are.
We both help others, and hurt them.
We support others, and let them down.
We strengthen our families, and weaken them.
We rejoice in the love of others, and trade upon it.
We build each other up, and drag each other down by jealousy
and envy.

We are sinners:
all the love and health in us is weakened by our sickness and sin.
Only you can make us face up to the truth.
Only you can cleanse and heal and remake us.
We put ourselves in your hands now,
in the Name of Jesus Christ our Saviour. *Amen.*

Thanksgiving and Dedication

Lord God, heavenly King, we thank you that you have made us
male and female, together in your image. Thank you for the
contribution each makes to the richness of life, and the completion
found in each other. For friendship, courtship and marriage, we
thank you.

You call us to play a part in your great creative purpose, so you
grant us the gift of children. Thank you for the ways in which the
young need the old, and the old the young. For all the blessings of
family life, we thank you.

We thank you for Jesus our Lord, called to remain single for the
sake of the kingdom. Thank you for the freedom he found to love,
and to give of himself to all, even to the sacrifice of the Cross.

We thank you for all the resources for loving, so freely given to us.

For every marriage holding firm despite tension and turmoil; for every household enabling each member to grow in faith and maturity, in love and forgiveness and trust; for every single person giving love and glad service to others, we thank you.

And now: what God has joined together, we will not separate;
husbands will honour wives, and wives husbands;
children will respect parents, and parents children;
we who are single will give ourselves in service;
so that we all learn from you how to love each other.
For this is your will, made plain in Jesus.
So be it, Lord. *Amen.*

Sixteenth Sunday after Pentecost

Adoration

God, our creator, Father and Lord,
maker of all that is and is to be,
we adore you.
Yours is the authority, the majesty, the splendour;
yet in your Son, our Lord Jesus Christ,
we see your graciousness, humility and compassion.
We would not dare to approach you,
but for Christ's revelation of your love and care for us.
The honour due to you
is beyond the expression of our finite minds,
but we know that you understand all that we cannot say,
and in such trust we offer up our praise;
in the Name of Jesus Christ our Lord. *Amen.*

Confession

Our heavenly Father,
we confess that we have fallen far short of what you would have us
    be.
We have trusted in ourselves, and not in your fatherly goodness.
We have not acknowledged that whatever strength and intellect
    we have comes from you.
We have found it hard to submit to authority, both temporal and
    spiritual,
forgetting that in your authority is perfect freedom.
As we contemplate the overwhelming troubles of the world
    around us,
we have to confess how little effort we have made
to understand our fellow men and women
or to promote the cause of justice and peace.

We humbly seek your forgiveness and renewing power,
that we may live our lives more worthily;
for the sake of Jesus Christ, the Saviour of the world. *Amen.*

Thanksgiving and Dedication

Eternal God, the creator and ruler of all,
we give you thanks and praise.
Your Son came among us, full of grace and truth,
to rescue us from sin and death,
the one mediator between God and mankind,
who sacrificed himself upon the Cross as a ransom for all the
    world.
You raised him from the dead
and gave him all authority in heaven and on earth,
that in the Name of Jesus every knee should bow;
and you have sent your Holy Spirit upon us
to enable us to live according to your will.

Today we thank you especially
for people in authority who use their power aright,
and for all who work for our good.
We are grateful for the times when you have enabled us to do right
and have saved us from our own waywardness.
Above all, we thank you that you never forget your covenant with
    us;
and so we dedicate ourselves to a deeper commitment to you
and a greater zeal in our reading of your word
and our meditation upon your will for us.
Help us to accept your authority in our lives,
for it is the authority of love.
In Christ's Name we ask it. *Amen.*

Seventeenth Sunday after Pentecost

Adoration and Confession

Almighty God, creator of all that is, you are worthy of all praise,
for not only is the universe vast, varied, and full of wonder,
it is also consistent and reliable,
it works to your pattern,
it obeys your laws.
We can depend on the regular succession of tides, of seasons, of
    day and night, of life and death.
In creation and in redemption, your word is your deed.
We worship and adore you.

Lord Jesus Christ, the Word become flesh, you are worthy of all
    praise,
for your deeds were always consistent with your words.
You told others to be humble in spirit –
and you lived a life of humble service,
even to the extent of kneeling and washing the disciples' feet.
You told others to trust in God and obey his will –
and you walked the way of obedience and faith,
from the wilderness to Gethsemane,
from Gethsemane to Calvary.
You told others to love and forgive –
and you loved to the end
and forgave those who nailed you to the Cross.
We worship and adore you.

....

Forgive us, Lord Jesus,
that our deeds so often fail to match up with our words.
Like Peter, we are ready to boast our allegiance one moment
and to deny you the next.
We have failed in humble service,
we have failed in trust and obedience,
we have failed in love and forgiveness.
Forgive us, Lord Jesus.

As you renewed Peter and called him to shepherd your sheep, we pray that you will renew us and recall us to your service, so that we may praise you not only with our lips but in our lives; for your sake and to your glory. *Amen.*

Thanksgiving and Dedication

We thank you, Lord,
for the beauty of the fruitful earth in the glorious colours of
    autumn,
for families and friends,
for good neighbours and the community in which we live,
for the fellowship of the Church.

Above all, we thank you for our Lord Jesus Christ,
the Word made flesh –
for his life and example,
for his death and resurrection,
for his faith that his friends, strengthened by the Holy Spirit,
would carry on his work.

We thank you for the faith we have, for it is your gift.
We pray that it may find expression in the life of the Church,
as we build each other up,
and in the life of the community,
as we encourage the young, cheer the old,
visit the sick and help the needy.

Lord, we are your servants.
We pray that, not only by the words we speak,
but by the lives we live,
we may spread the Gospel of Christ
and win others for him;
for his sake. *Amen.*

Eighteenth Sunday after Pentecost

Adoration

Almighty God, we worship and adore you.
Out of chaos and gloom you have brought order and light,
out of the darkness of night you create each new day.

We praise you, Father,
that in the resurrection of your Son, Jesus Christ,
you have demonstrated so clearly
your power over evil, sin and death.

We rejoice that we can gather together in his Name,
and in the power of the Spirit,
to share the joy of his triumph
in the face of pain and suffering,
and to praise you
for your greatness, your faithfulness, and your love.

Almighty God, we worship and adore you
in the Name of Jesus Christ our Lord. *Amen.*

Confession

Father, you have called us together as your people, and made
available to us all the resources of your grace. Forgive us for the
times when our lives have not openly showed our love for you, or a
loving concern for others.

We confess that we have failed to make worship the first of our
priorities and that we have been reluctant to offer you in praise
and service the gifts and talents you have freely bestowed on us.
We recognize how easily we have slipped into an attitude of selfish
ingratitude, which has dulled our sensitivity to the needs of others
and the demands of your kingdom.

Eighteenth Sunday after Pentecost

We pray that our failures may not become our burden. Grant us
your forgiveness to make us free, and a fresh vision of our calling
to follow you; through Jesus Christ our Lord. *Amen.*

Thanksgiving and Dedication

For the creation of the world with all its variety, beauty, colour,
and activity; almighty Father,
we give you thanks.

For the gift of Jesus Christ to be our Saviour; for his lowly birth,
his loving ministry, his suffering and death, and the triumph of his
resurrection; almighty Father,
we give you thanks.

For the Church throughout the world, and for its ministers,
layworkers, and members; for all mission and service being carried
out now in the Name of Jesus Christ; almighty Father,
we give you thanks.

For those Christians who remain bold in the face of persecution,
whose lives are a living testimony to the power of the Holy Spirit;
almighty Father,
we give you thanks.

For the opportunities which are presented to us to use our talents,
time, and possessions to your glory in the Church and in the world;
almighty Father,
we give you thanks.

Father almighty, we re-dedicate ourselves to you.
Make us loyal and dependable, loving and obedient,
faithful to you in every part of our lives;
for the sake of Jesus Christ our Lord. *Amen.*

Nineteenth Sunday after Pentecost

Adoration

We come in reverence to your house, Lord:
we come in humility to this holy place.

We have learned of your purity and holiness;
you are enthroned in glory, high and lifted up.

We rejoice that you have bridged the gap between us,
that from your throne, high and lifted up,
you came in Christ, and laid your glory by.

And so we come, not only in reverence and humility,
but also in the knowledge of your active love.

We come in faith,
for you have stretched out your hand to us,
and we put our hands in yours,
not only our God, but our Father;
through Jesus Christ our Lord. *Amen.*

Confession

We have our good days, Lord, when all seems well, and we are
sure of our faith.

We confess that we have our bad days, Lord, when all seems ill,
and doubts assail us.

We confess our preoccupation with the immediate, our concern
for today and tomorrow.

Forgive us that we forget that we are your children, that in Christ
we are more than conquerors.

We know in our hearts that you have always been faithful.
We pray that you will help us to a faith which is founded on rock,
the rock of our salvation;
through Jesus Christ our Lord. *Amen.*

Nineteenth Sunday after Pentecost

Thanksgiving and Dedication

We thank you, Father, for your eternal witness to the world,
that in no generation have you been left without faithful servants.

We thank you for your Church universal:
    for its corporate witness to a secular world;
    for its ministry of teaching, healing, and preaching;
    for its service to the poor, the lonely, and the neglected.

We thank you for the faith of your people
    who sustain your work and witness,
    people steadfast in their faith, and sensitive to your promptings.
Above all, we thank you for Jesus, the ground of all our hopes,
    the Church's living Head.
    For he lived the life of faith,
    obedient to your call, and loyal to your command.
    Trusting in you alone, he worked among us
    and died on the Cross for our salvation,
    revealing your boundless grace.
    We thank you for raising him from the dead,
    exalting him to your right hand
    and sending us the Holy Spirit
    who helps us to live by faith in you.

We would grow in faith, Father,
running a good race,
confident of our high calling,
faithful in your service;
for the sake of Jesus Christ our Lord. *Amen.*

Twentieth Sunday after Pentecost

Adoration

Almighty God, so wise and powerful
that none can stand against you,
we praise you.
You are stronger than earthquakes, storms and raging seas:
open our eyes to an awareness of your power.
You know the secrets of the atom and the vastness of outer space:
open our minds to your wisdom and creativity.
Your love is so deep that you know the innermost secrets of all
　　your children:
open our hearts to you as friend.

Powerful and loving God,
you bring all things under your rule.
All monarchs and presidents,
all ministers and officers,
owe their allegiance to you.
So we ask to see your glory,
a glory shown supremely in your Son
to whom you gave all authority,
and a glory which can be reflected
in the lives of all whom Jesus calls.

Lord God, you are our strength and our salvation.
We proclaim and adore your glorious Name;
through Jesus Christ our Lord. *Amen.*

Confession

Lord God, we confess our lack of faith, especially when we have
doubted your power to achieve your purposes. Help us to put our
trust in your strength, and to know that you still work through
those committed to you.

We confess our ignorance. When we do not understand, and are tempted not to seek to understand, help us to search for and to recognize the truth.

We confess our sense of loneliness and failure. When we feel that there is no one who can help us with our problems, help us to turn to you, and to know that there are those who can keep confidence.

We confess a sense of disillusionment with those in positions of power. Help us to have a realistic awareness of what to expect from earthly authorities, but to set no limits to what you can achieve when working through others and through us.

So, Father, help us, inadequate though we are, to know that we can draw upon your strength, and in that strength can be agents of your glory; through your Son, Jesus Christ our Lord. *Amen.*

Thanksgiving and Dedication

We thank you, Lord God,
for our place in the world you have created:
that we are citizens both of earth and of heaven.
We thank you for your mighty act of creation
which supplies our food, our fuel, and our physical protection,
for work and for social activity.

We thank you for Jesus,
whose human life and social relationships,
whose suffering and death and resurrection,
demonstrate a higher quality of love and fellowship
than what is merely human.
We thank you for the Church,
established to continue this fellowship
through the Holy Spirit.

We are grateful for the benefits of national and local government,
and for the work of those who make and uphold our laws.
We thank you for the opportunities we have to express opinions,
to make choices, and to vote.

Lord God, as we strive to earn a living,
to develop healthy relationships,
and to exercise our choices as citizens,
we re-dedicate ourselves to you;

and we pray that, in the power of your Spirit,
we may also demonstrate the life
of citizens of heaven;
through Jesus Christ our Lord. *Amen.*

Twenty-first Sunday after Pentecost

Adoration

Strong and wise God,
we love you because you first loved us.
We cannot count all your blessings,
and your goodness cannot be exhausted.
On your power our lives depend,
and the least of us flourishes through your care.
In the Name of your Son,
you hear our quietest prayers;
by the help of your Spirit,
our requests are uttered and answered.
In word and sacrament,
you assure us of forgiveness
and nourish us by grace.
You surround us with a cloud of witnesses
and make us brave through the example of your saints.
You remind us of those who endured to the end,
looking only to Jesus,
the pioneer and perfecter of our faith.
You show us the quiet signs
of affection and neighbourliness.
We bless you for these glimpses of yourself,
creator and Father of all,
and we worship you in the Spirit;
through Jesus Christ our Lord. *Amen.*

Confession

Merciful Father,
we have heard your commission
to preach Christ to every creature,
and we have busied ourselves in carrying it out.

We have been concerned
with cleverness of presentation
and invincibility of argument.
We have multiplied our organizations,
published our good tidings,
and counted our successes.

Forgive us, Lord,
that we have gone in our own strength;
that we have preached ourselves;
that we have drawn attention
to our church or society or cause,
rather than to Jesus, the crucified one.
Draw us closer to him,
and put his spirit within us.
Conform us to his heart and mind,
who for the sake of the joy before him
endured the Cross.
Mark all our work
with the unmistakable signs of his peace and love.
Make us faithful servants,
and, by your forgiveness,
free us to live for Jesus' sake. *Amen.*

Thanksgiving and Dedication

God our heavenly Father,
we thank you for the refreshment we receive
as we celebrate, Sunday by Sunday,
the day of creation,
the day of resurrection,
the day the Spirit came upon the Church.

You divide day from night,
and invite us to live as children of the light.
You raised Jesus from the dead
and offer us life in all its fullness.
You gather disciples together,
and set us on fire
to proclaim your power in every age.

We thank you that our life and ministry
are set in a time of challenge;
that our faith is tested,
our ways rough and uncharted;
and we thank you for your promise
to save us in the time of trial.
Thus you teach us to depend on your grace,
and to live close to you
in humility and hope.

Draw us closer to those whom you love:
attune our ears to the cry of the poor;
open our eyes to see Christ in those around us.
Make us your instruments of peace and reconciliation
in your way and in your time.
And do not leave us alone
until we come to your eternal kingdom;
through Jesus Christ our Lord. *Amen.*

Twenty-second Sunday after Pentecost *(Year 1)*

See the prayers for 6th Sunday after Epiphany *(Year 2)*

Twenty-second Sunday after Pentecost *(Year 2)*

See the prayers for 6th Sunday after Epiphany *(Year 1)*

Twenty-third Sunday after Pentecost *(Year 1)*

See the prayers for 5th Sunday after Epiphany *(Year 2)*

Twenty-third Sunday after Pentecost *(Year 2)*

See the prayers for 5th Sunday after Epiphany (Year 1)

Watchnight

Adoration

We praise you, eternal God:
you are beyond all time and all space;
you were present before you created the world,
and you will exist when the world is no more.

A thousand years in your sight are like a day that is past,
or as an hour in the night;

you are from everlasting to everlasting;
you made the earth, and the sky, and the sea,
the hills and the rivers,
all that shall be when we are no more:

for we are like the grass of the field
which grows for a day, and is cut;
we wither and die;
but around us are the abiding hills,
the rivers and streams, the over-arching sky.

All the world is yours;
but you are beyond it,
beyond all our imaginings.

Eternal God, we praise you. *Amen.*

Confession

Lord God, our heavenly Father, as we come to the end of another
    year,
we confess our sins before you:

we have not loved you as we should have done;
we have not worked for you as we should have done;
we have not spoken out for you as we should have done.

Watchnight

We have been like servants who were not ready for the master's coming: we have thought too much of ourselves, and too little of you. We ask you to forgive us all our sins: our envy of others, our laziness in your service, our greediness, our outbursts of temper, our care about money, our secret lechery, our pride.

May we feel the joy of your forgiving power as we begin this new year: give us such a sense of your mercy and your goodness, that we may put our guilt and shame behind us and give our lives to your service; through Jesus Christ our Lord. *Amen*.

Collect

Almighty and everlasting God,
constant and faithful and unchanging,
your goodness and mercy have followed us
all the days of our life:
grant that as we enter this new year,
trusting in your unfailing love,
we may serve you with grateful and obedient hearts;
through Jesus Christ our Lord. *Amen*.

Thanksgiving and Dedication

God our Father, our sustainer and guide,
we thank you for bringing us safely to the end of another year.
You have provided for us and blessed us,
and we give you thanks for all the benefits which we have received;
for happy days and peaceful nights;
for the beauty of creation, and the changing seasons of the year;
for friends and laughter;
for the beauty of art, and the joy of work well done;
for food, and health;
for the knowledge of your truth, revealed in the life and death, the
    resurrection and ascension of Jesus Christ, your Son;
for the hope that makes us free in the glorious liberty of the
    children of God.

Tonight we dedicate ourselves again to your service.
May this coming year be spent in accordance with your will:

make us your servants, with our lights burning ready for your
   coming,
and may we be wise stewards,
using what years remain to us to your honour and glory;
so that in the day of your coming in majesty,
at the end of all years,
we may receive the glad word,
enter into your joy,
and sit down with you in glory;
through our Saviour Jesus Christ. *Amen.*

Aldersgate Sunday

Adoration

Glory be to you, God the Father,
for you have found a way for the recovery of lost sinners.
Glory be to you, God the Son,
for you have loved us and washed us from our sins.
Glory be to you, God the Holy Spirit,
for by the mighty working of your grace
you have turned our hearts from sin to God.

To God the Father, God the Son, and God the Holy Spirit,
be glory and blessing and honour and might for ever and ever.
  Amen.

Aldersgate Sunday

Confession

Almighty God, our heavenly Father,
we confess with shame that we have sinned against you
and against our fellows.
We have not loved you
with all our heart and soul and mind and strength;
we have not loved our neighbours as ourselves.

But while we were yet helpless, Christ died for the ungodly;
and we trust in Christ, Christ alone, for salvation.

Grant to us, we pray, the assurance that Christ has taken away *our*
   sins and saved *us* from the law of sin and death.
We ask it in his Name. *Amen.*

Collect

Almighty God, you plucked as a brand from the burning your
   servant John Wesley, that he might kindle the flame of love in
   our hearts and illuminate our minds:
grant to us, we pray, such a warming of our hearts,
that we, being set afire by holy love,
may spread its flame to the uttermost parts of the earth;
through Jesus Christ our Lord. *Amen.*

Thanksgiving and Dedication

Eternal God, Maker of heaven and earth, eternal God our Father,
as we thank you for creating us in your image,
so we praise you still more for sending your Son
to restore what we had lost.

We thank you for his lowly birth, his precious passion,
his mighty resurrection and his glorious ascension;
we praise you that he has gone to prepare a place for us,
that where he is, we may also ascend
and reign with him in glory.

We thank you for sending to us his Holy Spirit,
who enables us to call you Father.

180

We thank you that in every age you have raised up faithful
    witnesses to your truth,
and at this time we thank you especially for all that you wrought
    through John Wesley,
who by the preaching of the Gospel
brought many to accept your precious and very great promise
that they might be partakers of the divine nature.

We thank you that you have raised up the people called
    Methodists
to go as labourers into the harvest to continue this work;
and we dedicate ourselves afresh to your service.
Empower us, we pray, by your Holy Spirit;
and bring us all to heaven;
through Jesus Christ our Lord. *Amen.*

Education Sunday

See the prayers for 9th Sunday before Easter, the day upon which
Education Sunday is now commonly observed.

All Saints' Day

Adoration

Mighty God, you are Father of a great family,
a family made up of people from every age,
drawn from the four winds and from every continent and island.
Your community transcends time and space.
Beings still unknown to us, yet known to you,
bright beings of superior powers, and human beings blessed with
    hope
join in your great service.

Within your family each has a place in your love
and no one is neglected or overlooked.
Your care extends to every member
and every member plays a part in your perpetual praise.
Earthly and unearthly music blend,
nature and grace combine,
earth and heaven agree,
within the bright orbit of your shining.

May we, with all your saints on earth,
now sing your praises in concert with the saints in heaven;
through Jesus Christ our Lord. *Amen.*

Confession

We confess to God almighty, Father, Son, and Holy Spirit, before
    all the company of heaven, and to each other, that we have
    sinned through our own fault.

We have been proud in our own conceit instead of taking a lower
    place within the company of those who are being perfected by
    love.

We have not always revered God's holiness by respecting one another; we have been lacking in courtesy and consideration for others.

We have not always honoured the memory of those whom we have loved and lost; we have despaired of life without them instead of believing in the communion of saints.

We pray that we may be forgiven and enabled, once again, to accept our call to be saints on earth; through the merits of Jesus Christ our Saviour. *Amen.*

Thanksgiving and Dedication

God our Father, creator of the universe, our maker and preserver, we thank you
  for making us unique individuals, able to find fulfilment in mutual appreciation, service and love;

  for redeeming us through the life and death, the resurrection and ascension of our Lord Jesus Christ, so that our destiny is not here but beyond;

  for surrounding us with a great cloud of witnesses who encourage us by their faith and perseverance to the end;

  for promising us in baptism and holy communion a share in the resurrection of Christ and, through him, reunion with those whom we love who are temporarily beyond our sight;

  for setting us in a larger world and wider fellowship through the mystical communion of all saints.

Help us to live in Christian confidence, believing that nothing in life or death is able to separate us from your love in Christ, assured that your loving wisdom and almighty power will keep us in your good purpose. Grant that, in the darkness of death, light perpetual may shine upon us.

These prayers we offer through Jesus Christ our Lord, who lives and reigns with you in the unity of the Holy Spirit, one God, world without end. *Amen.*

Remembrance Sunday

Adoration

Incomparable God, Father of each one of us,
we praise and adore you.
Your love is unending,
your mercy limitless,
your power infinite,
your grace unbounded.
You alone give life its full and true direction;
you bring good out of evil,
life out of death,
and hope out of despair.
We are amazed that you continue to concern yourself with us,
despite our deep and constant unworthiness of you.
Faithful, gracious Father,
we offer you our praise and adoration
with reverent, humble, and thankful hearts;
in the Name of Jesus Christ our Lord. *Amen.*

Confession

Father, our own human history condemns us,
making plain our sinfulness.
We are unable to live together in harmony;
our self-assertion, greed, ignorance and prejudice
ensure that peace is always short-lived.
We let pride and patriotism blind and deafen us
while justice and mercy go unheeded.
We abuse your gift of knowledge:
we do not use our technology for good,
so often choosing destructive and inhuman courses instead.

Even within your Church,
we have failed to live out the Gospel of peace,

184

failed to show people their true worth,
failed by our unfaithfulness in praying for the world,
failed by accepting injustice and so increasing tension.

Father, we need your forgiveness.
Despite the immensity of our sin, set us free from it;
and may the knowledge of your constant forgiving grace
result in our striving for peace
and actively seeking the good of all;
for Christ's sake. *Amen.*

Collect

Almighty Father,
you call your children
to live as brothers and sisters,
in love and harmony,
and have given your Son to be our Saviour,
the Prince of Peace:
grant that we, who are called by his Name,
may yield our lives to your service,
and strive for reconciliation, understanding, and peace
in all our relationships;
for the sake of Jesus Christ our Lord. *Amen.*

Thanksgiving and Dedication

We give thanks, God our Father,
for the world you have created and given into our care.
We thank you for the survival of the earth
and the continued existence of humanity on it.

We give thanks that,
despite our cruelty and violence as a race,
we know also the power of mercy and compassion;
in the face of hatred and lies,
we know something of love and truth;
in the midst of death and war,
we recognize peace and life as attractive.
Gracious God, giver and revealer of all good,
we thank you and praise you.

We give thanks, Father, for Jesus Christ,
the Lord of life, the conqueror of death,
the giver of eternal life and peace and hope.

We give thanks, Father, for the Holy Spirit,
for his ceaseless revelation of Christ's powerful Gospel,
in the world, in the Church, and in us.

We give thanks, Father,
for all people who, by their lives and deaths,
bear witness to a hatred of war and a true love of peace.

Father, we dedicate ourselves again to you.
Grant us grace to live out the Gospel of peace,
and use us, empowered by your Holy Spirit,
to shape our earthly society
into the likeness of your heavenly kingdom;
through Jesus Christ our Lord. *Amen.*

Christian Citizenship Sunday

Adoration

Lord God, before whom every knee shall bow
and whom every tongue shall praise,
we come to worship you.
There is no light in our lives or in the life of the world
that does not come from you.

In your presence
the morning stars first sang together
and the sons of God shouted for joy,
and in your hand is the destiny of all life.
You are the King and the Judge,
but also our Saviour and Friend.
We bring our adoration and praise,
imperfect though it is,
and ask that you will accept our service of worship;
through Jesus Christ our Lord. *Amen.*

Confession

Lord God, every good thing in our lives comes from you;
and yet we confess with shame
that we have not lived together as your children
and shared the gifts that you have given us.
So often our lives have reflected not your glory but our own
    selfishness.

Forgive us, Lord, if we have loved only those who have loved us,
if we have sought our own pleasure
and disregarded the needs of our fellows.
Forgive us if we have been unkind in our judgments,
quick to condemn and slow to forgive.
And forgive us if we have given in to our worst
and made it difficult for others to live up to their best.

Lord God, if we have come into your presence bitter and cynical,
send us out rejoicing and full of gratitude;
and make us men and women with pure and great hearts
so that we may see our God;
for Christ's sake. *Amen.*

Collect

Almighty God,
your Son Jesus Christ
came not to be served, but to serve,
and to give his life a ransom for many:

help us to love others as he loved us,
and make us responsible citizens of earth,
as in Christ we are made citizens of heaven;
for his sake. *Amen.*

Thanksgiving and Dedication

God our Father, we thank you for creating the world
and for sending your Son to redeem us from our sin.
By the way he lived and the way he died
he demonstrated the glorious power of love.
By his mighty resurrection and ascension
he has conquered sin and death.
By sending your Holy Spirit on the Church
you enable us to live as Christ's disciples
and to serve you in the Church and in the world.

We thank you, Father, that you have called us together
to build the City of God.
In this great task may no one in our fellowship
feel useless or unloved, lonely or unwanted.
Grant us a vision of your world as it might be –
a world of justice, brotherhood and peace,
founded not on force but on love.
Lord, hear the prayers of our hearts
as we pledge our time and our energy and our thought
to make this world what you intend it to be.

Send your Spirit into the dark places
of the world, our nation and our lives,
carrying faith to the doubting,
hope to the fearful, and strength to the weak.
Fill our lives with your love
and help us to pass on that love to others.
So let your kingdom come and your will be done
on earth as it is in heaven;
for the sake of Jesus Christ our Lord. *Amen.*

Overseas Missions

Adoration

Almighty God, our heavenly Father,
Lord of all creation,
giver of life and source of all justice and love,
we offer you our praise and our worship
on this your holy day.

Lord Jesus Christ, Son of the living God,
you are a light to all peoples, a beacon for the nations;
we offer you our praise and our worship
on this your day of resurrection.

Holy Spirit, by whose power
men and women of all nations are born again into God's kingdom,
we offer you our praise and our worship
on this day of your coming at Pentecost.

Almighty God, Father, Son, and Holy Spirit,
we join with all the Church on earth
and the Church in heaven
as we offer you our adoration and praise. *Amen.*

Confession

Almighty God, you loved the world so much
that you gave your only Son,
so that whoever believes in him should have eternal life.
We confess to you the narrowness of our vision and of our mission.
Often we are so preoccupied with local concerns
that we forget that we are part of a great world-wide fellowship of
    Christians.

Forgive us, Father, for our self-concern,
and grant us, through your Holy Spirit,

Overseas Missions

a wider vision of your Church and of your salvation;
for the sake of Jesus Christ our Lord. *Amen*.

Collect

Eternal God,
your Son commissioned his friends
to go into all the world
and make disciples of all nations:
hear our prayer for your universal Church,
that in every land the Gospel of Christ
may be boldly proclaimed and faithfully lived,
to the honour and glory of your Name;
through Jesus Christ our Lord. *Amen*.

Thanksgiving and Dedication

God and Father of humankind,
we thank you for the variety of races and of nations
which you have created to inhabit this planet.
We thank you that human beings are made in your image,
with the ability to think and to choose,
to do good or to do evil.

We thank you that you sent your Son Jesus Christ,
to live and to die and to rise again,
to be the Saviour of the world.

We thank you for your Holy Spirit,
who has raised up your Church
in all lands and among all nations.
We thank you for our sister churches
in all the continents of the world:
for their vigour and their growth,
and for the example they set before us.

We thank you for those from this country
who serve in the Church overseas (especially . . . . . .)
and for overseas ministers and laypeople
who are serving in this country (especially . . . . . .)

190

In gratitude, we offer you our lives
to be used in the service of your Church,
militant on earth, triumphant in heaven;
through Jesus Christ our Lord. *Amen.*

Harvest Thanksgiving

Adoration

Glory and honour are yours by right, Lord our God,
for you created all things, and by your will they exist.

We praise you, mighty creator,
whose glory is reflected in what you have made.
How perfect you are in power, in majesty, in wisdom!
How marvellous, how beautiful, how good is your creation!

Still more we praise you, gracious God,
because you have revealed yourself to us,
not only in what you have made,
but in the person of your Son, Jesus Christ.
In him we see the majesty and splendour
of your redeeming love.

Mighty creator, most merciful God,
we worship and adore you;
through Jesus Christ our Lord. *Amen.*

Harvest Thanksgiving

Confession

God our Father,
you are our creator, to whom we owe our every breath,
and you have set us in a world of beauty.

We confess with shame
that we have been unfaithful creatures,
unworthy stewards of creation.

Forgive us, we pray, our ingratitude,
our complacency, and our pride.
Pardon our selfishness,
our abuse and misuse of your bounty.

Grant that, with thankful hearts,
we may use your gifts aright,
and share what we have, by your mercy,
with all who need our help;
for the sake of Jesus Christ our Lord. *Amen.*

Collect

Almighty God, whose generous love
supplies us with the fruits of the earth in their seasons:
give us grace to be thankful for all your gifts,
to use them wisely,
and to share our plenty with others;
for the sake of Jesus Christ our Lord. *Amen.*

Thanksgiving and Dedication

We thank God our Father today
for the splendour and beauty of creation;
for the ordered succession of seasons;
for the love that made the world.

We give thanks to the Lord, for he is good;
and his mercy endures for ever.

We thank God for the good and fertile earth;
for the fruits of the earth in their seasons;
for the life that sustains our life;
for the food that we daily enjoy.

We give thanks to the Lord, for he is good;
and his mercy endures for ever.

We thank God for those whose labour
supplies our physical needs:
for those who harvest crops, those who transport them,
those who process them, those who sell them.

We give thanks to the Lord, for he is good;
and his mercy endures for ever.

We thank God for his greatest gift –
for Jesus, our Saviour and Lord;
for his living and dying and rising;
for redeeming the world by his love.

We give thanks to the Lord, for he is good;
and his mercy endures for ever.

We thank God for his Holy Spirit,
the Lord and the giver of life;
for the Church, which is God's new creation;
for the privilege which is ours of being part of it.

We give thanks to the Lord, for he is good;
and his mercy endures for ever.

Father, we thank you for your mighty acts
in the creation and redemption of the world;
and we offer ourselves to you in gratitude,
that we may serve you and our fellow men and women
joyfully and faithfully throughout our lives;
in the Name of Jesus Christ our Lord. *Amen.*

Church Anniversary

Adoration

Lord God, there is no God like you in heaven above or on earth
    beneath,
keeping covenant and showing steadfast love to your servants;
you have kept the promise which you made to our ancestors.
Heaven and the highest heaven cannot contain you;
how much less this house which we have built.

And yet to us as we gather here
this is indeed your house and the gate of heaven.
For all your faithfulness we praise you;
through Jesus Christ our Lord. *Amen*.

Confession

Almighty God, we come as into the courts of a King,
with awe and reverence;
we come also as into the home of a Father,
with love and confidence.

You are our King and you have the right to rule over us,
and we confess that even in the life of the Church itself
we have often sinned against you.
Sometimes we come to worship unprepared;
we have not read your Word
or prayed as we should have done during the week.
Sometimes we are unexpectant;
we do not expect that any great thing will happen.
Sometimes we lack zeal;
we do not long to spread the Gospel to others.
Sometimes we lack fellowship;
we do not want to get to know any other people.

But now that we are here,
you in your fatherly goodness are waiting to forgive us;
and so we gladly receive your pardon
and ask you to make us better Christians
and more loyal members of the Church;
for Christ's sake. *Amen.*

Collect

Almighty God, to whose glory we celebrate the anniversary of this
   church,
we give you thanks for the fellowship
of those who have worshipped in this place,
and we pray that all who seek you here may find you,
and being filled with the Holy Spirit may become a living temple,
a dwelling-place for your life-giving presence in the world.
We ask it through Jesus Christ our Lord. *Amen.*

Thanksgiving and Dedication

Father, almighty and everliving God, we praise you
that you made the world to resound to your glory.
You created men and women in your own image,
and gave them creative vision and inventive skill.

We praise you that, to restore what human sin had spoilt,
you sent to us your Son Jesus Christ.
He lived among us, and we saw his glory.
He defeated death by dying for us.
He was raised from the dead and exalted to heaven.

We praise you that through him you sent the Holy Spirit
to establish your Church on the foundation of the apostles and
   prophets,
with Jesus Christ as its chief corner-stone.

We praise you that this house of prayer has been built to your
   glory,
to help us on our way to the heavenly city,
the Jerusalem that is above,
where Christ will give his light for ever.

Accept us, we pray, as we dedicate ourselves to your service;
and grant that all who worship you in this place
may find here a foretaste of that heavenly city;
through Jesus Christ our Lord. *Amen.*